My name is

Track the letter and colour each picture when you have completed the matching page in your work book.

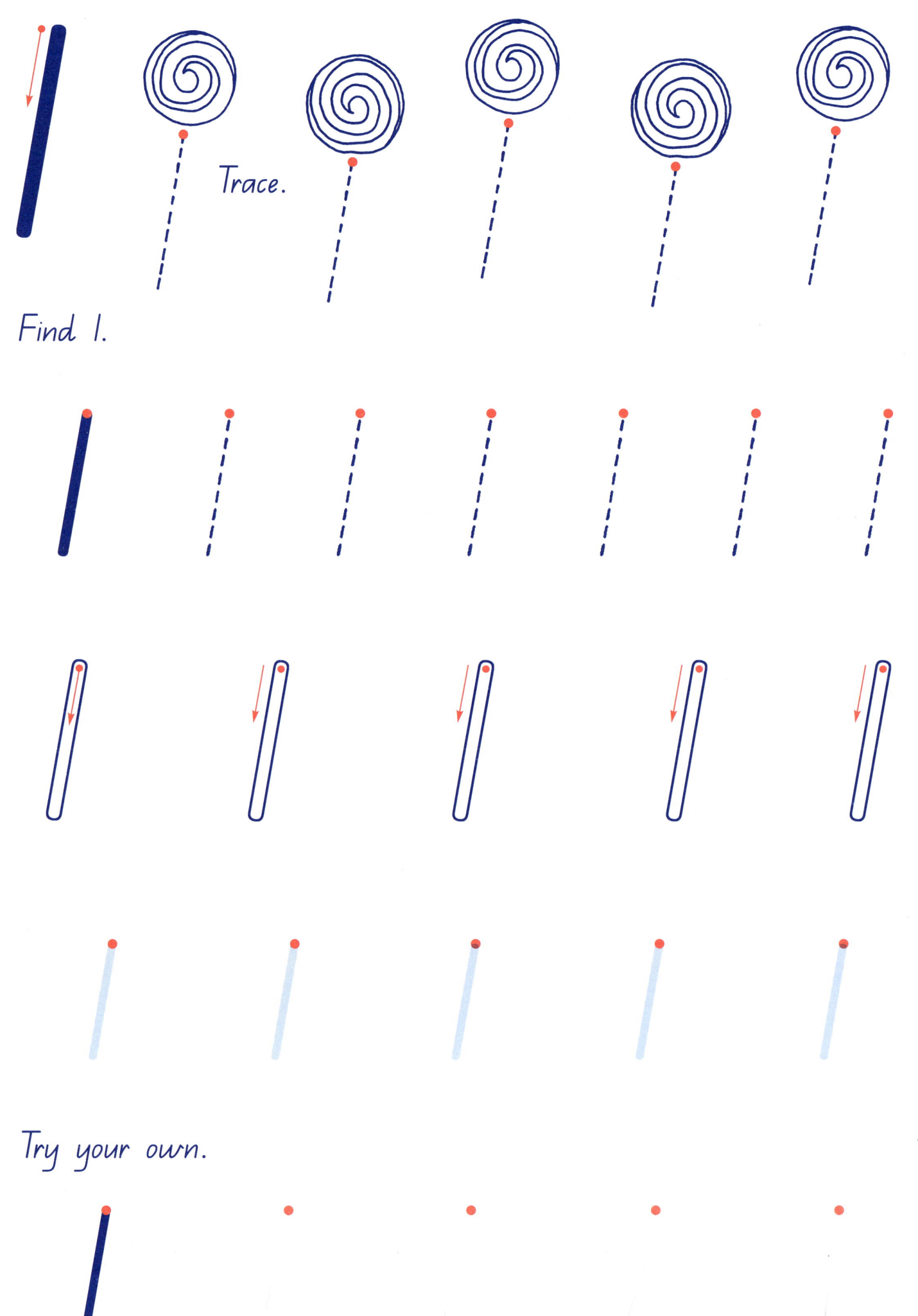

Trace.

Find 1.

Try your own.

a head and
body letter

lamp

Give the fairies their wands.

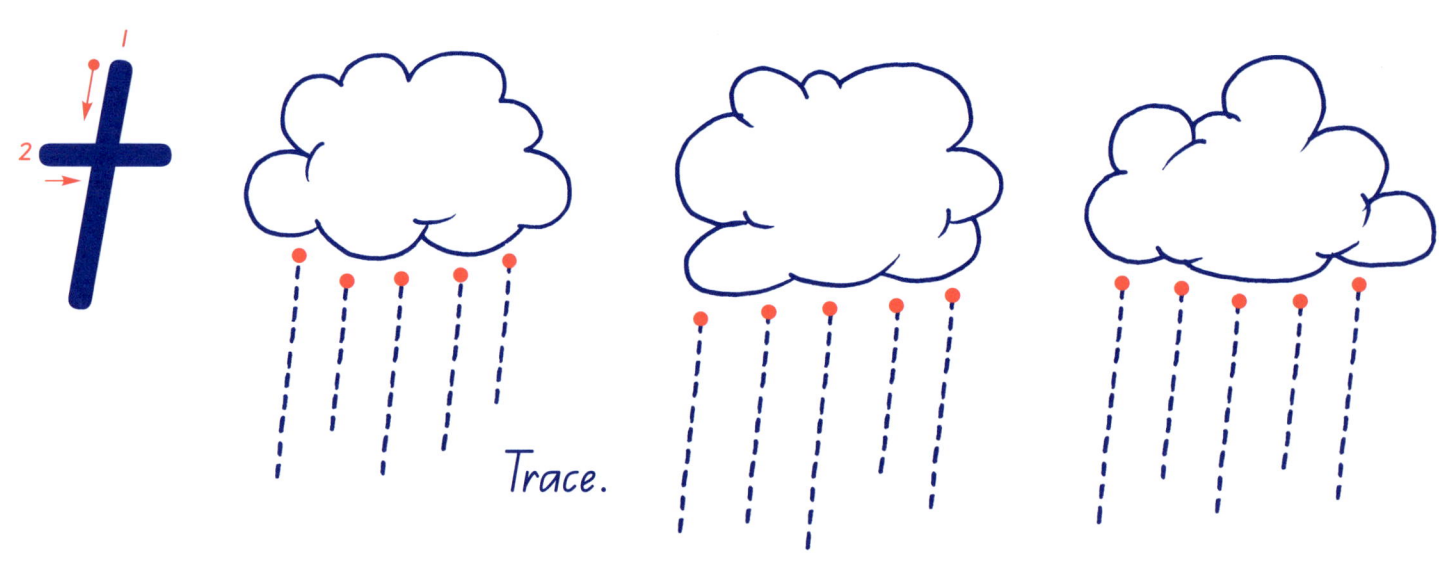

Trace.

Trace. Find t.

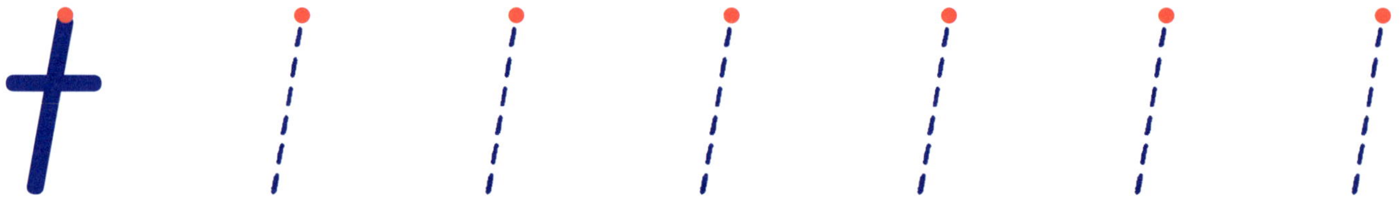

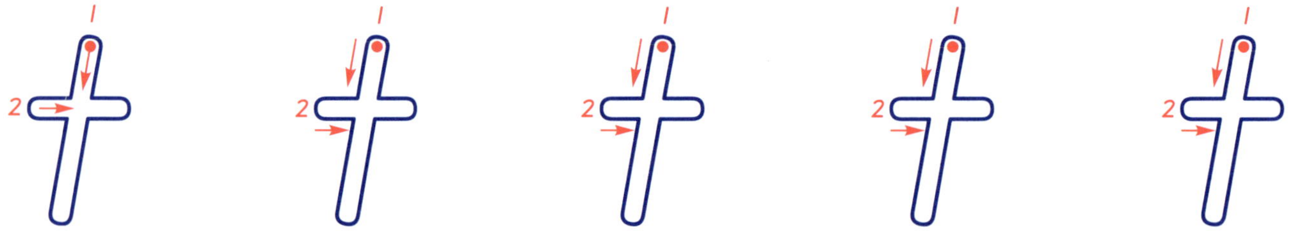

Try your own.

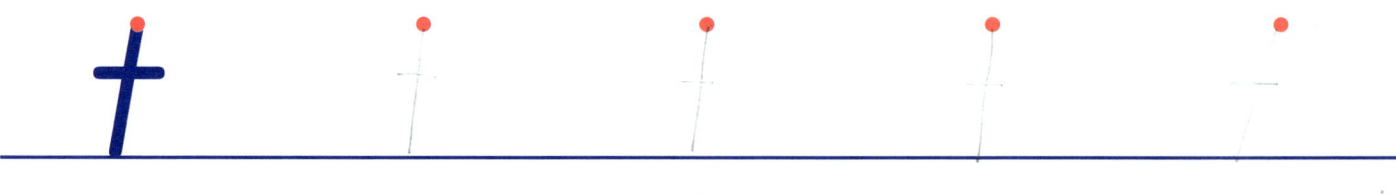

a head and body letter

tree

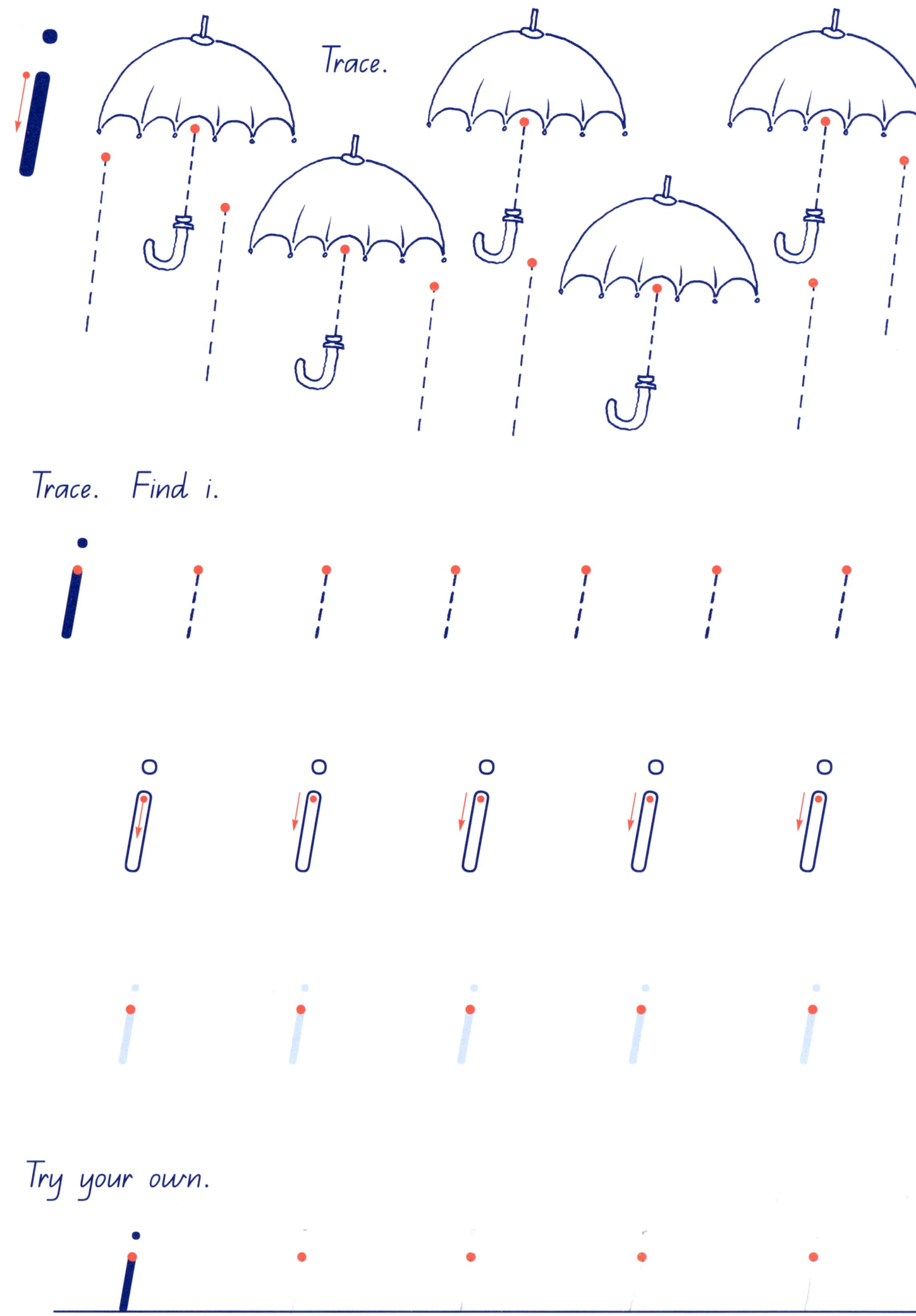

Trace.

Trace. Find i.

Try your own.

8

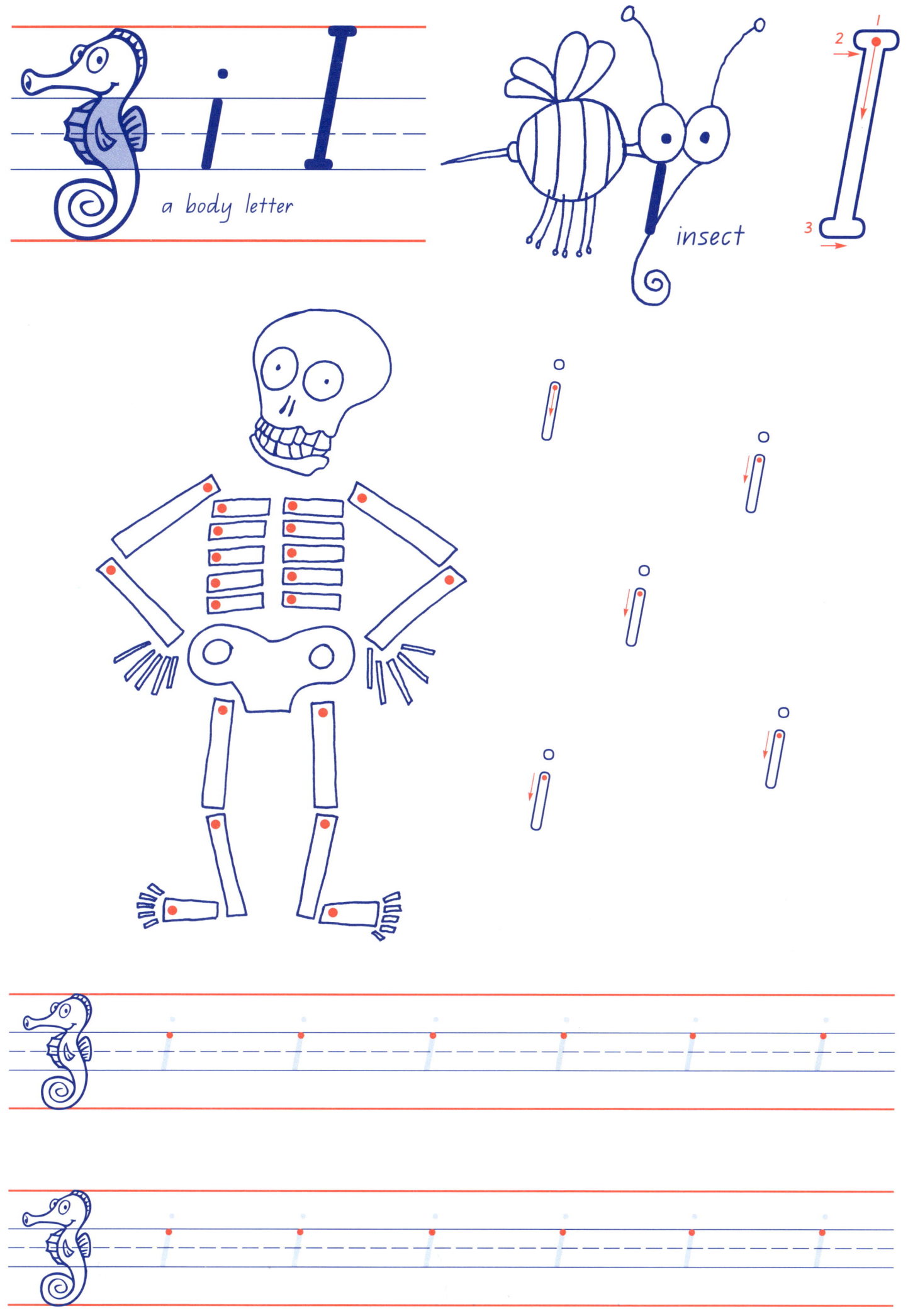

i I

a body letter

insect

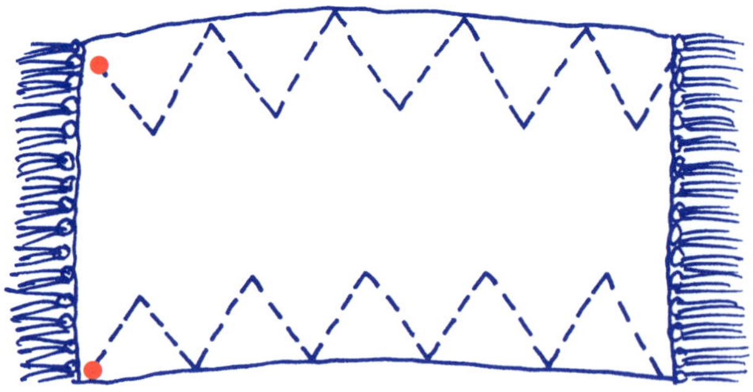

Trace.

BOING

Trace. Find x.

Try your own.

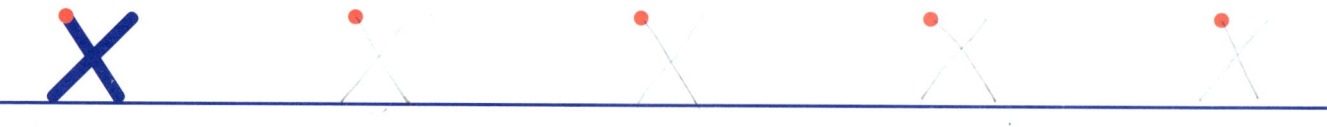

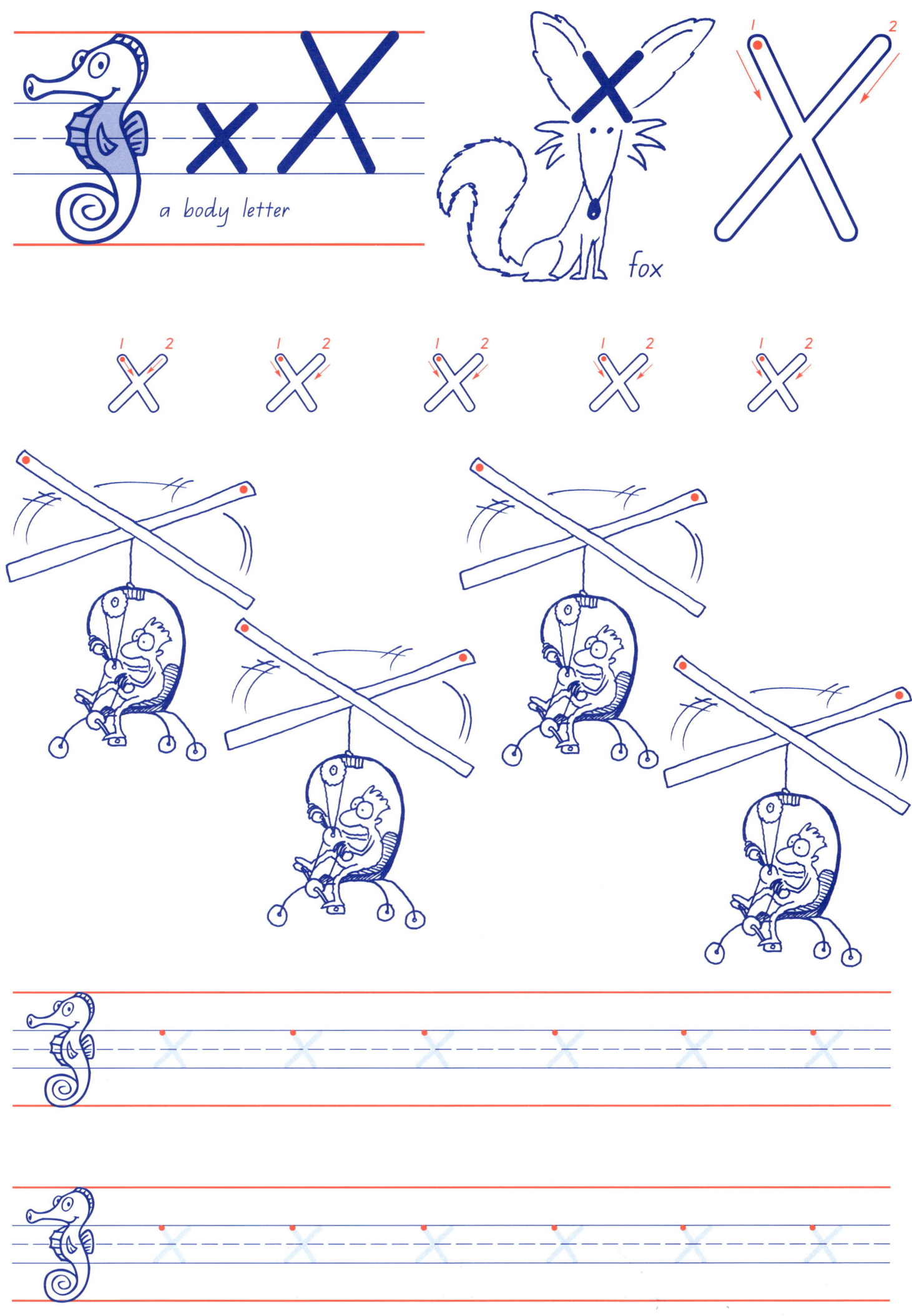

a body letter

fox

Z

Trace.

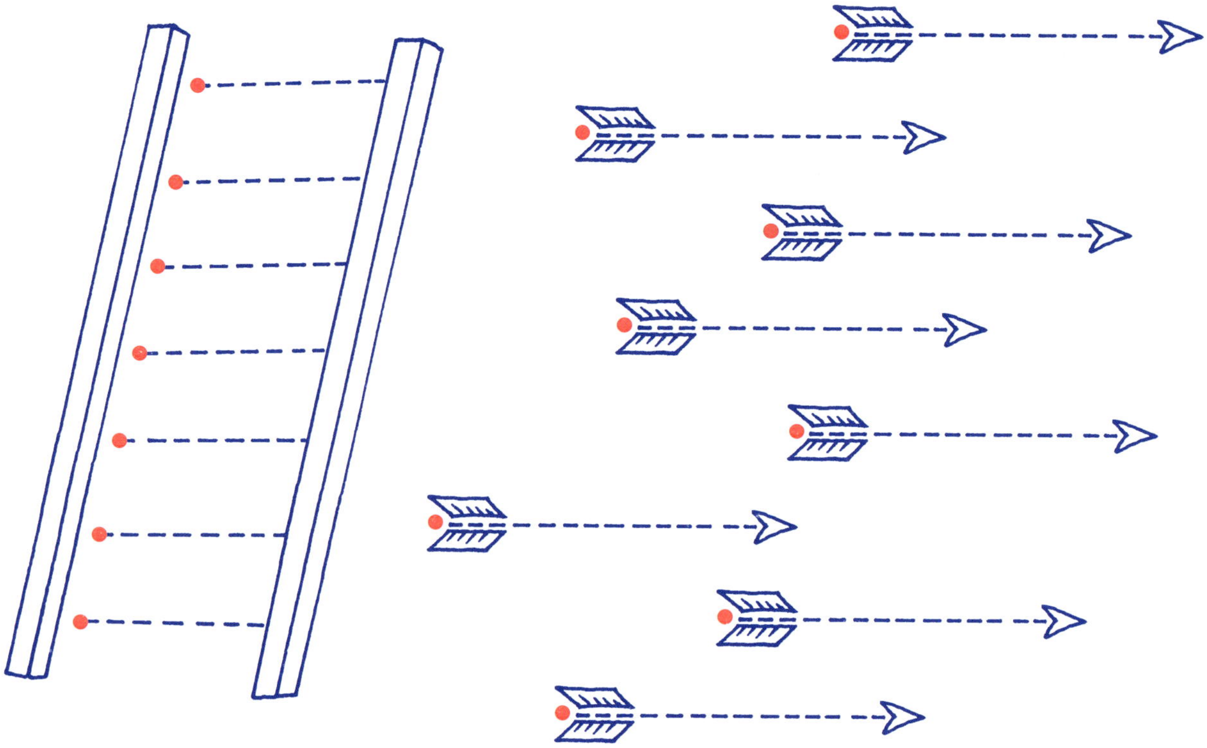

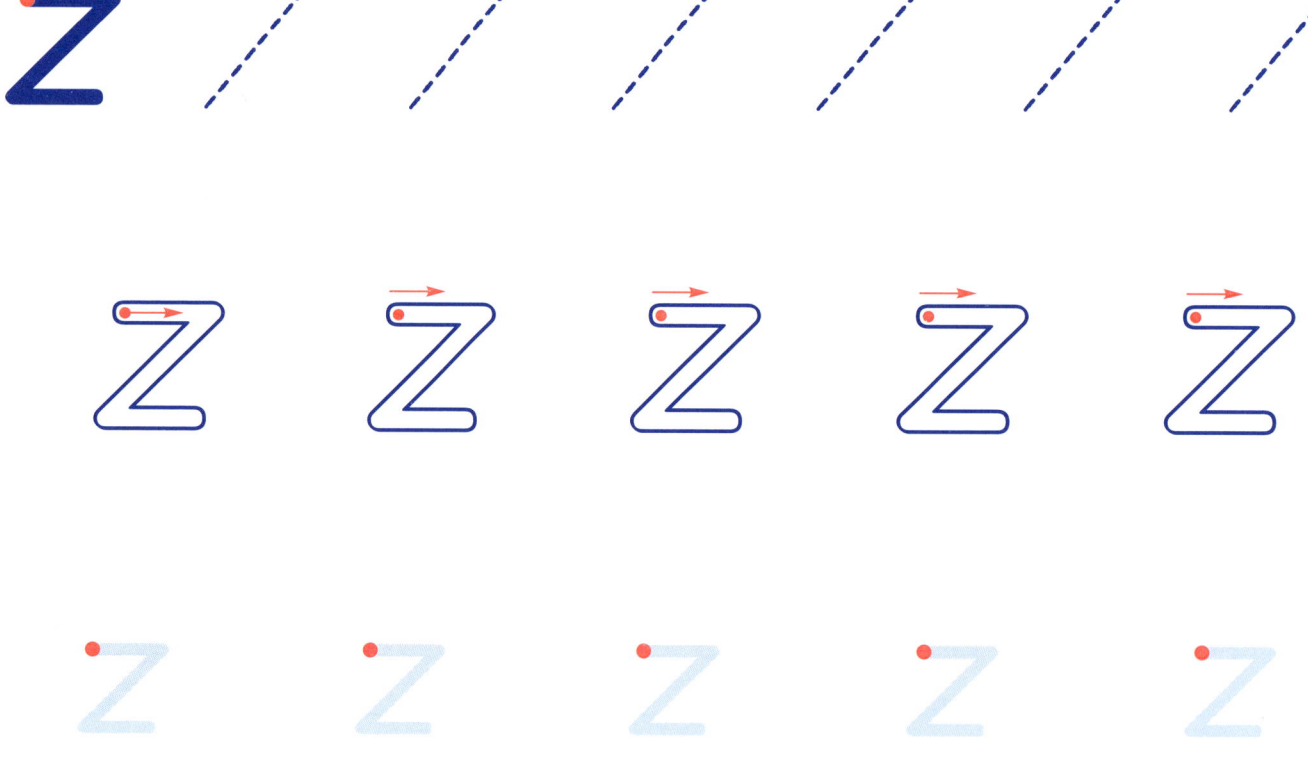

Find z.

Try your own.

a body letter

zebra

Trace.

Find f.

f

Try your own.

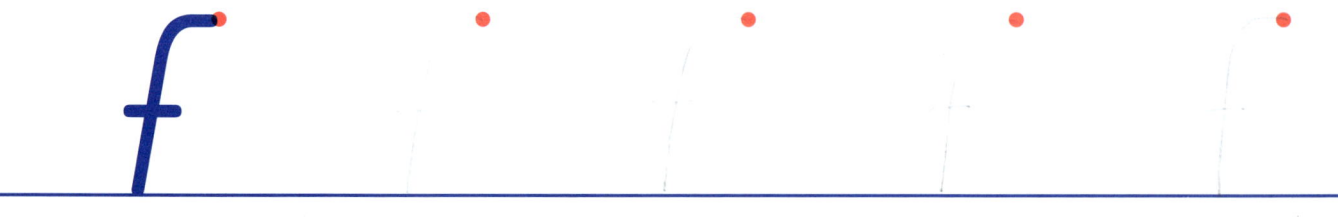

f F

a head and
body letter

fish

f f f f f

Trace Grandad's walking stick.

j

Trace.

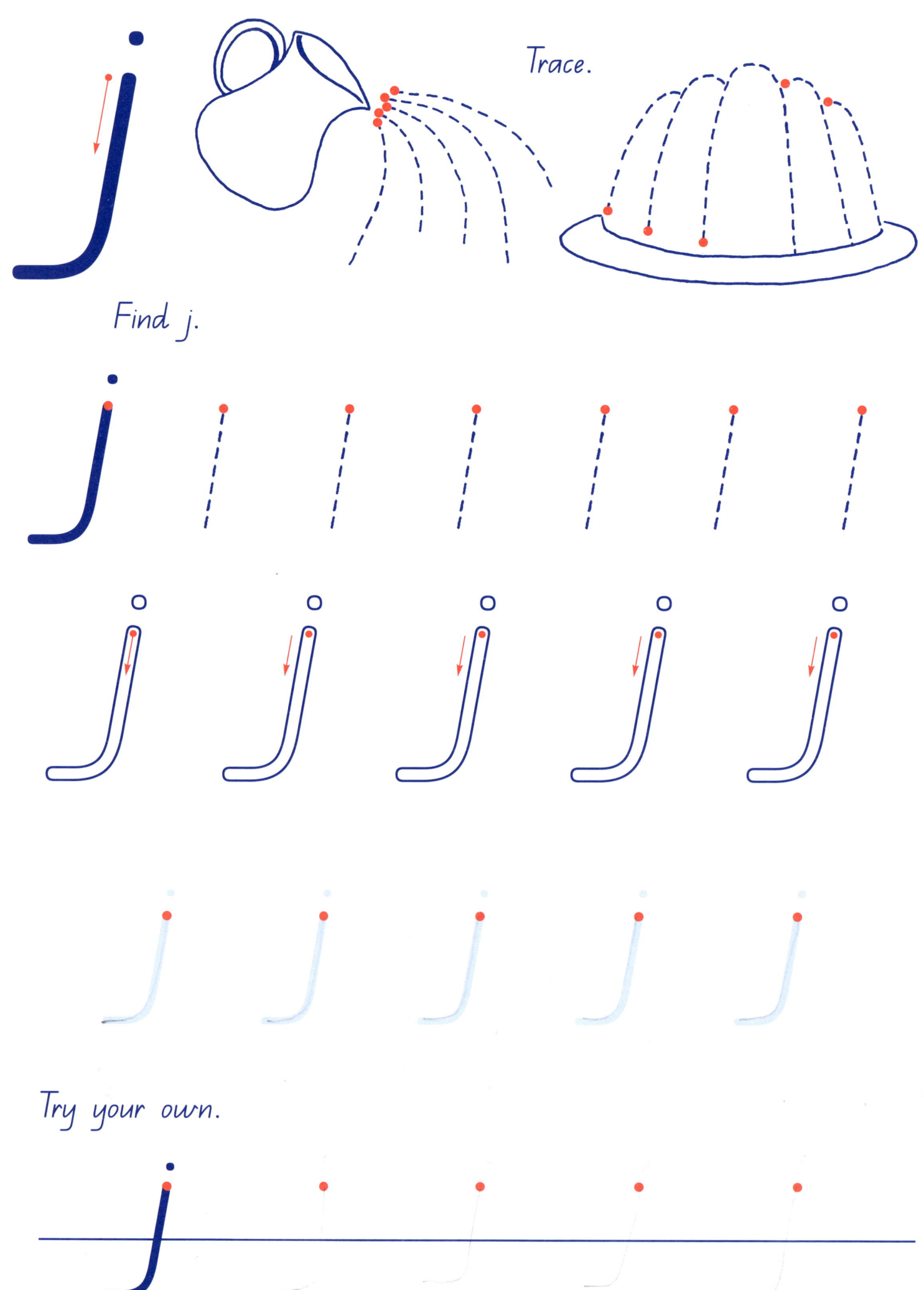

Find j.

Try your own.

16

a body and
tail letter

j j J

jet

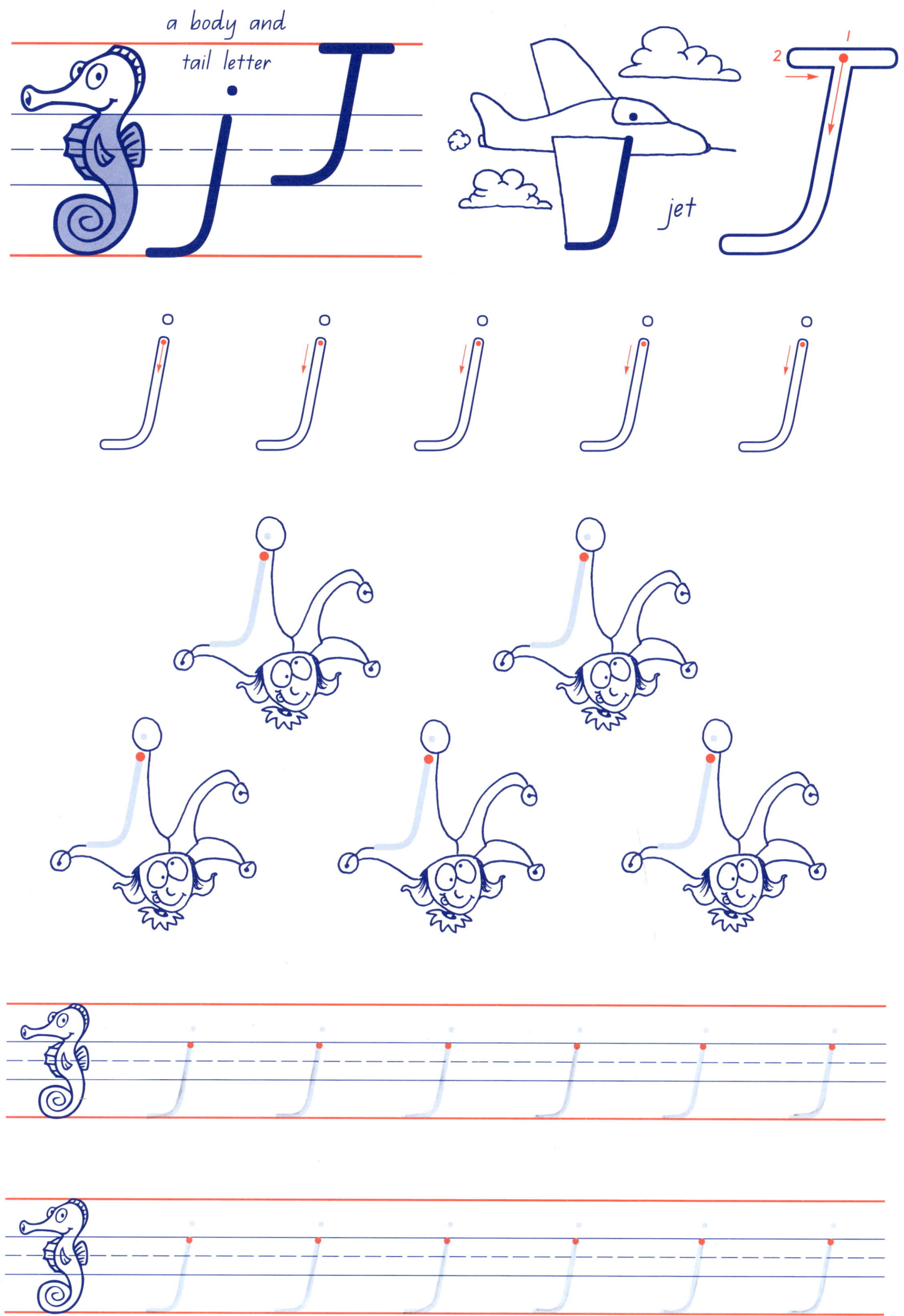

Trace.

Trace. Colour the wedges of cake.

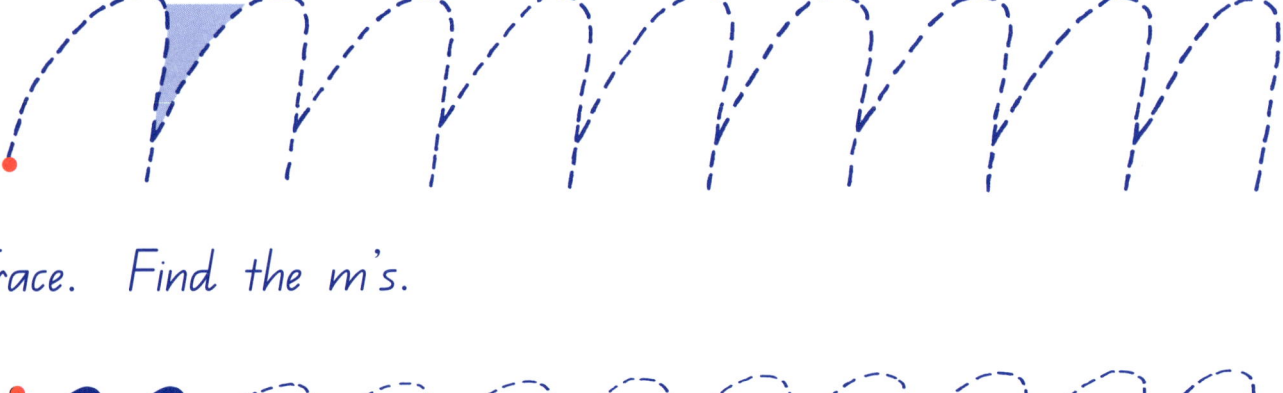

Trace. Find the m's.

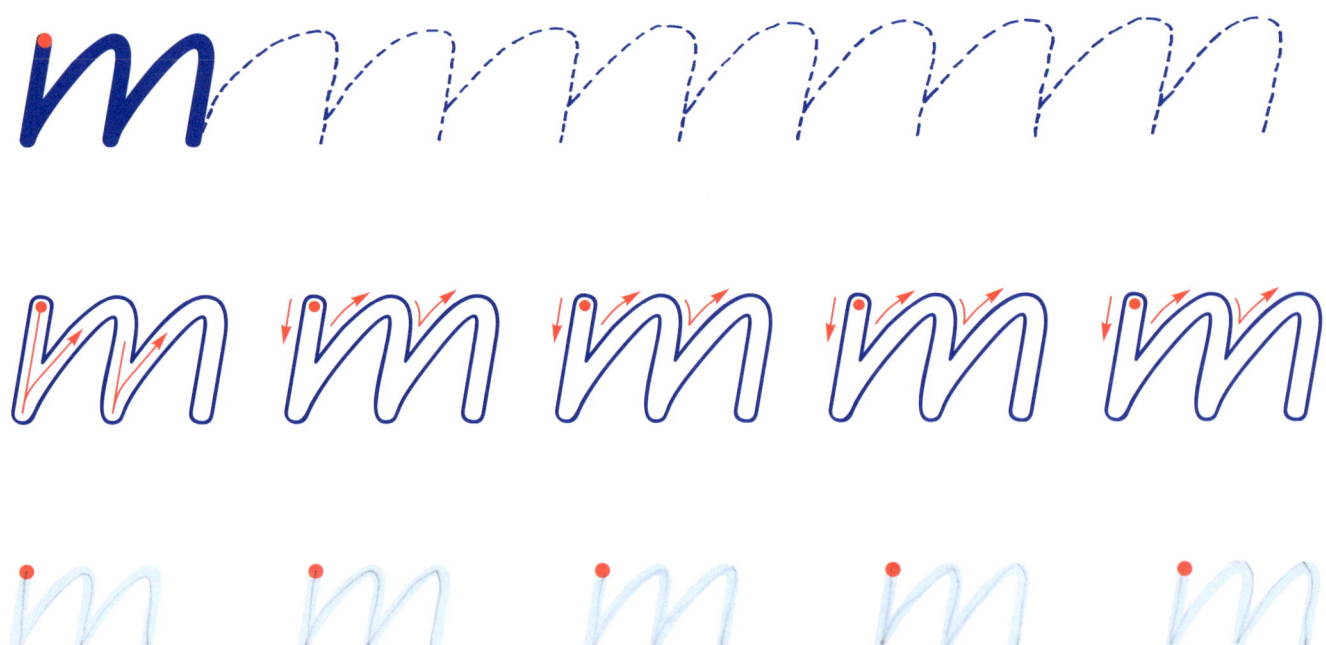

Try your own.

a body letter

mountains

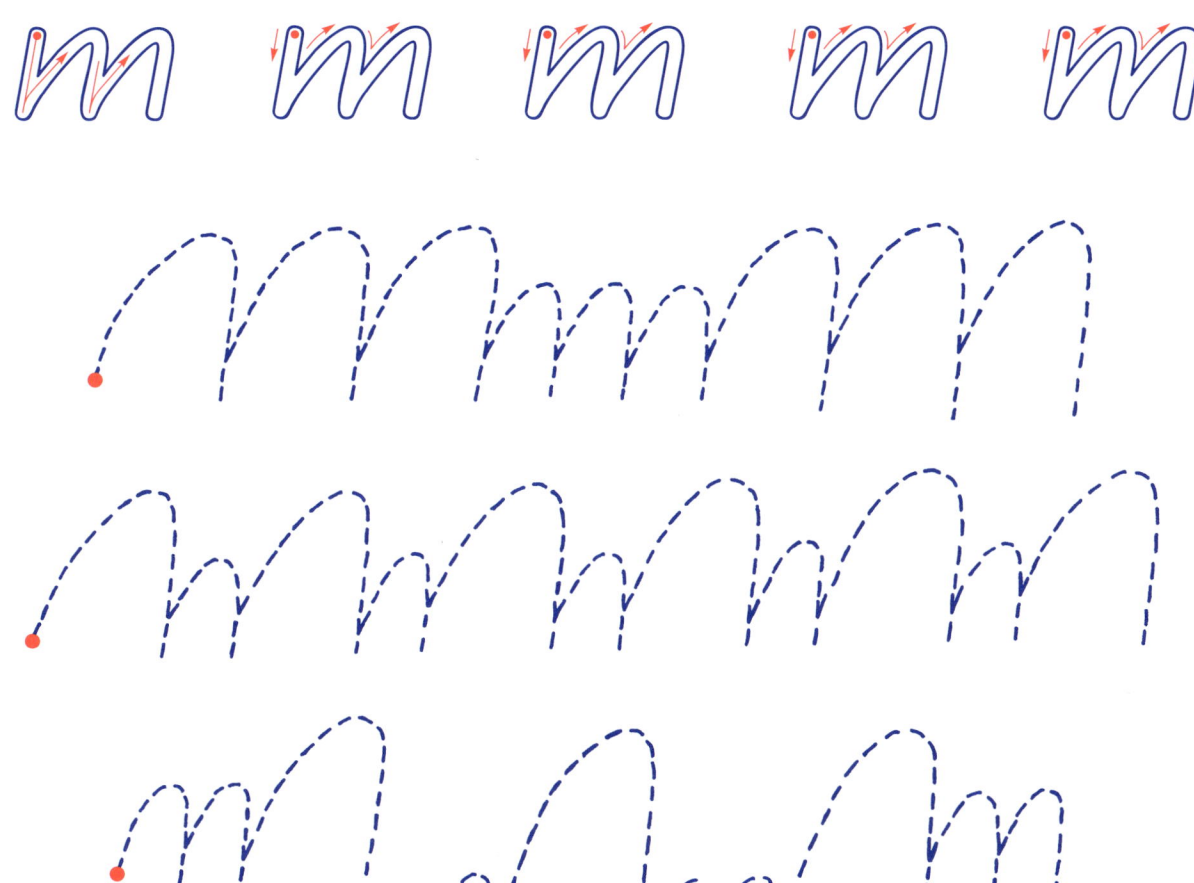

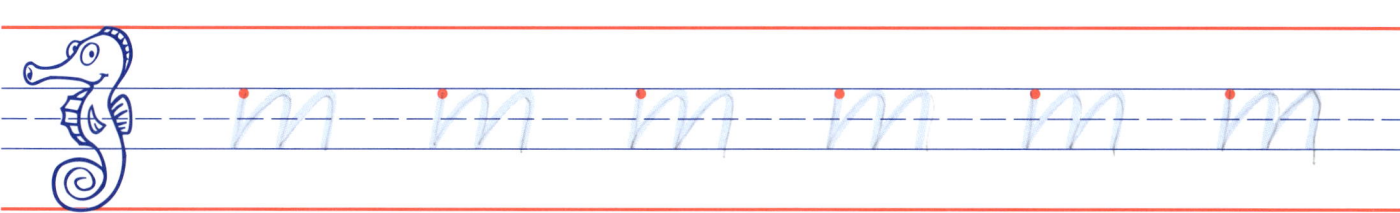

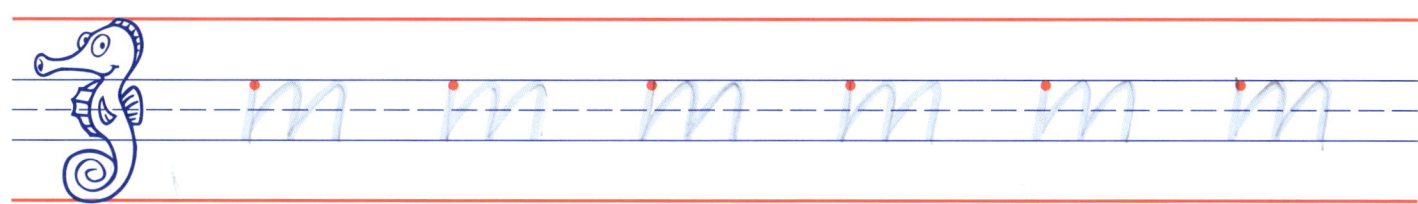

19

Track.

Trace the hops using 3 different colours.

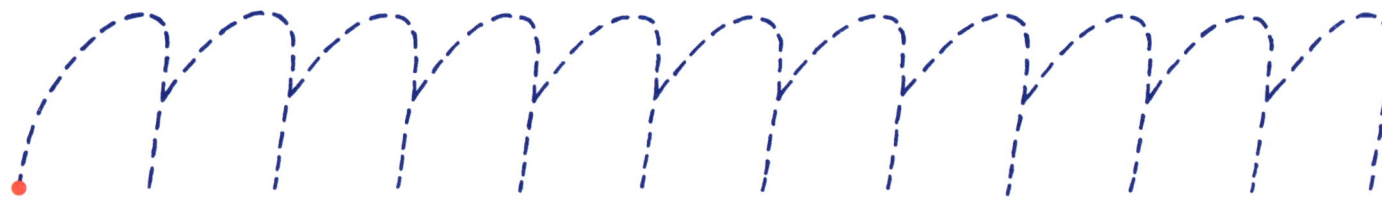

Trace. Find the n's.

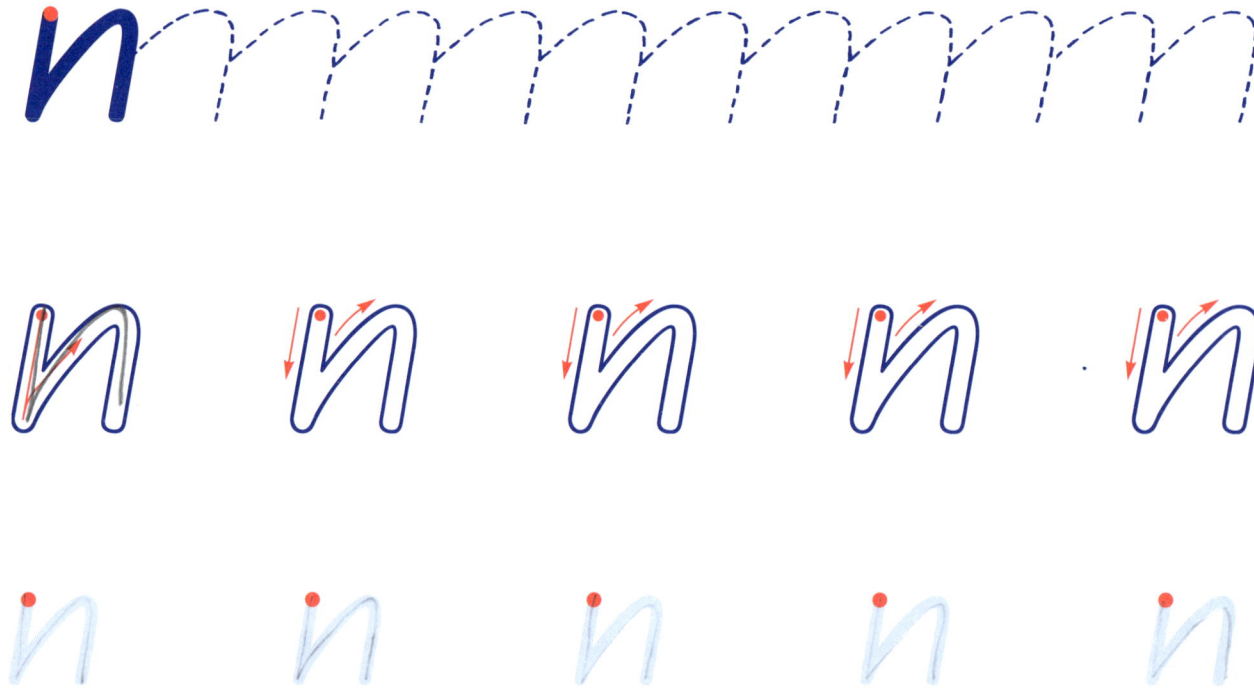

Try your own.

a body letter

nest

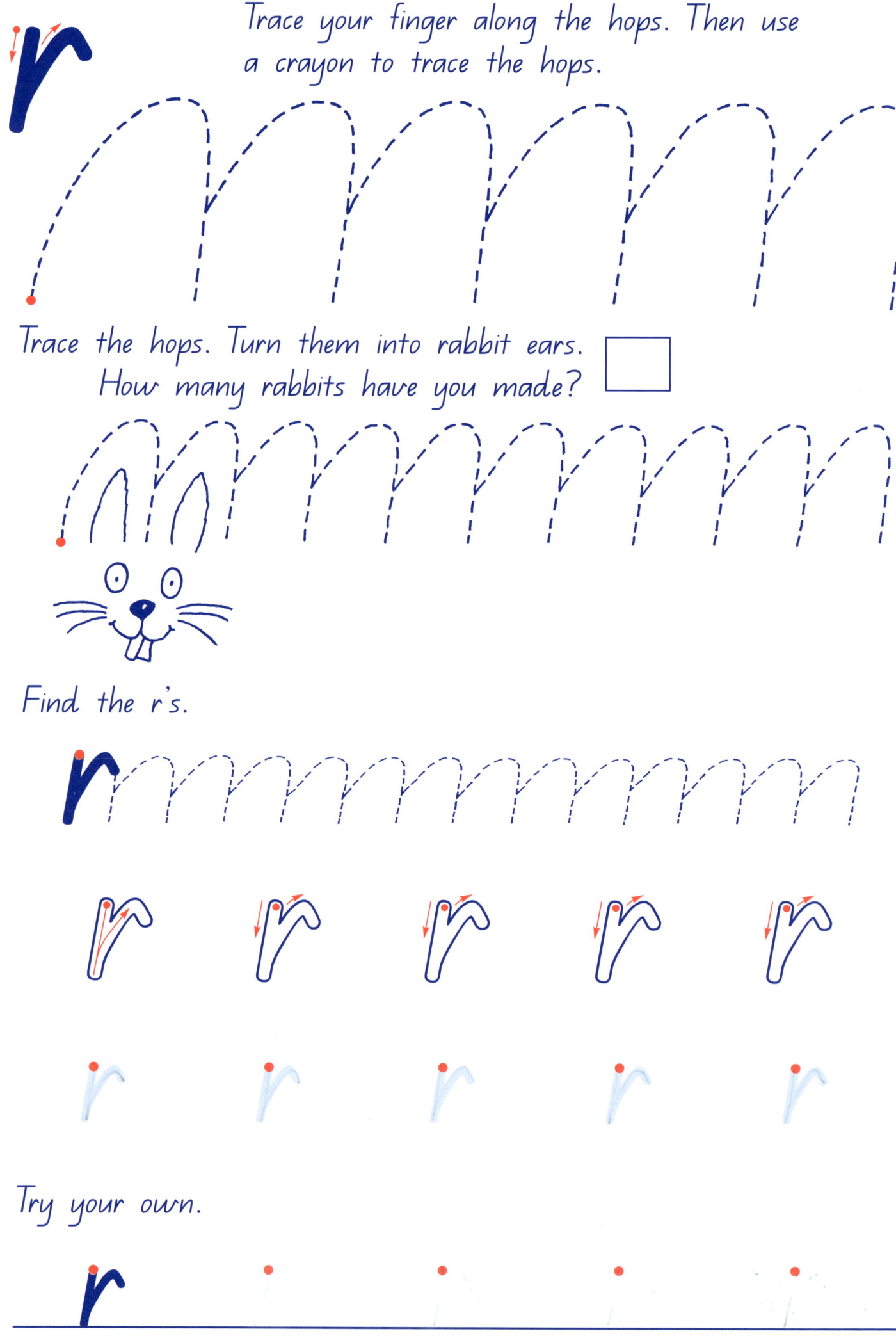

Trace your finger along the hops. Then use a crayon to trace the hops.

Trace the hops. Turn them into rabbit ears.
How many rabbits have you made?

Find the r's.

Try your own.

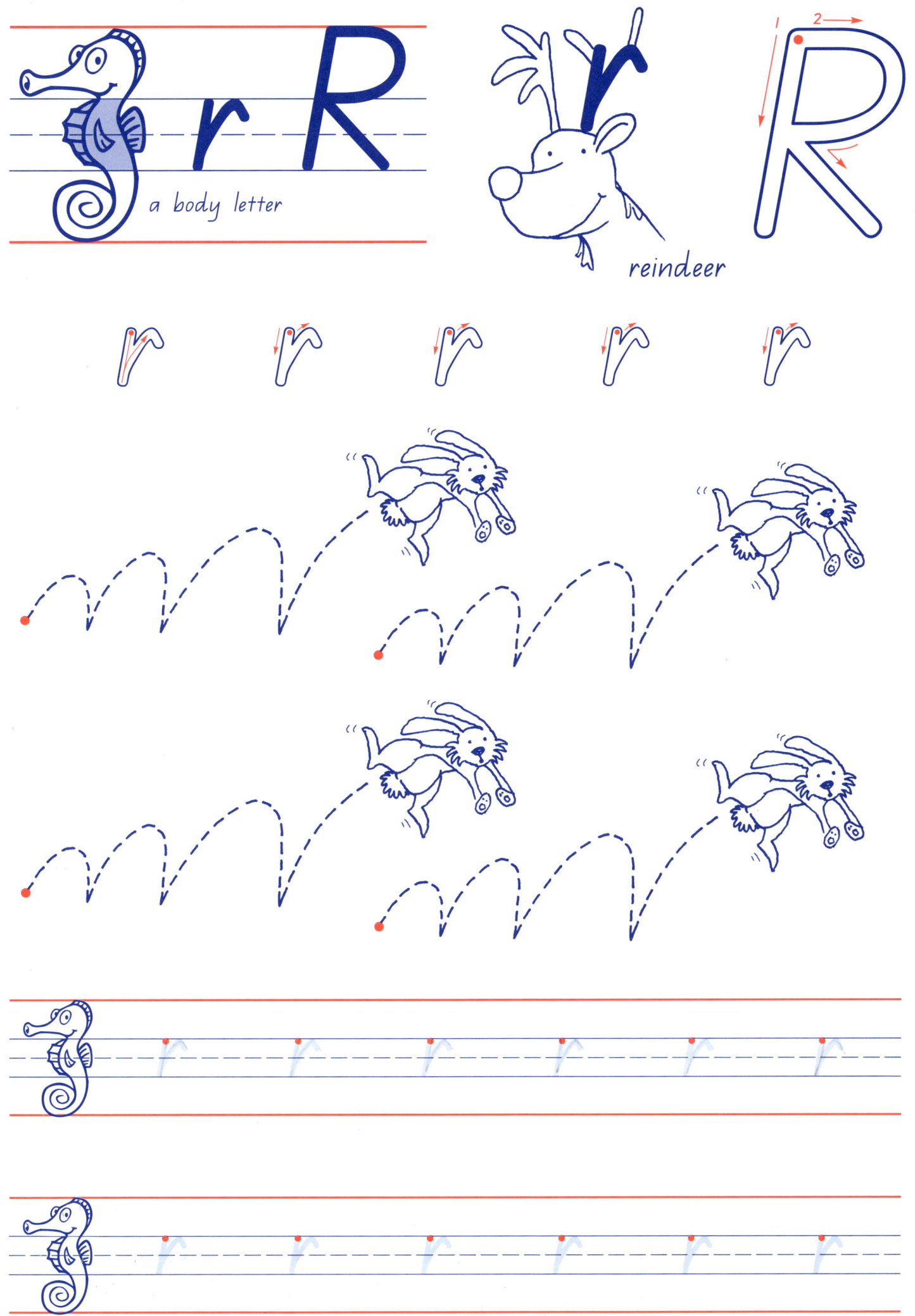

r R

a body letter

reindeer

h

Trace. Colour the wedges of cake.

Trace. Find the h's.

Trace.

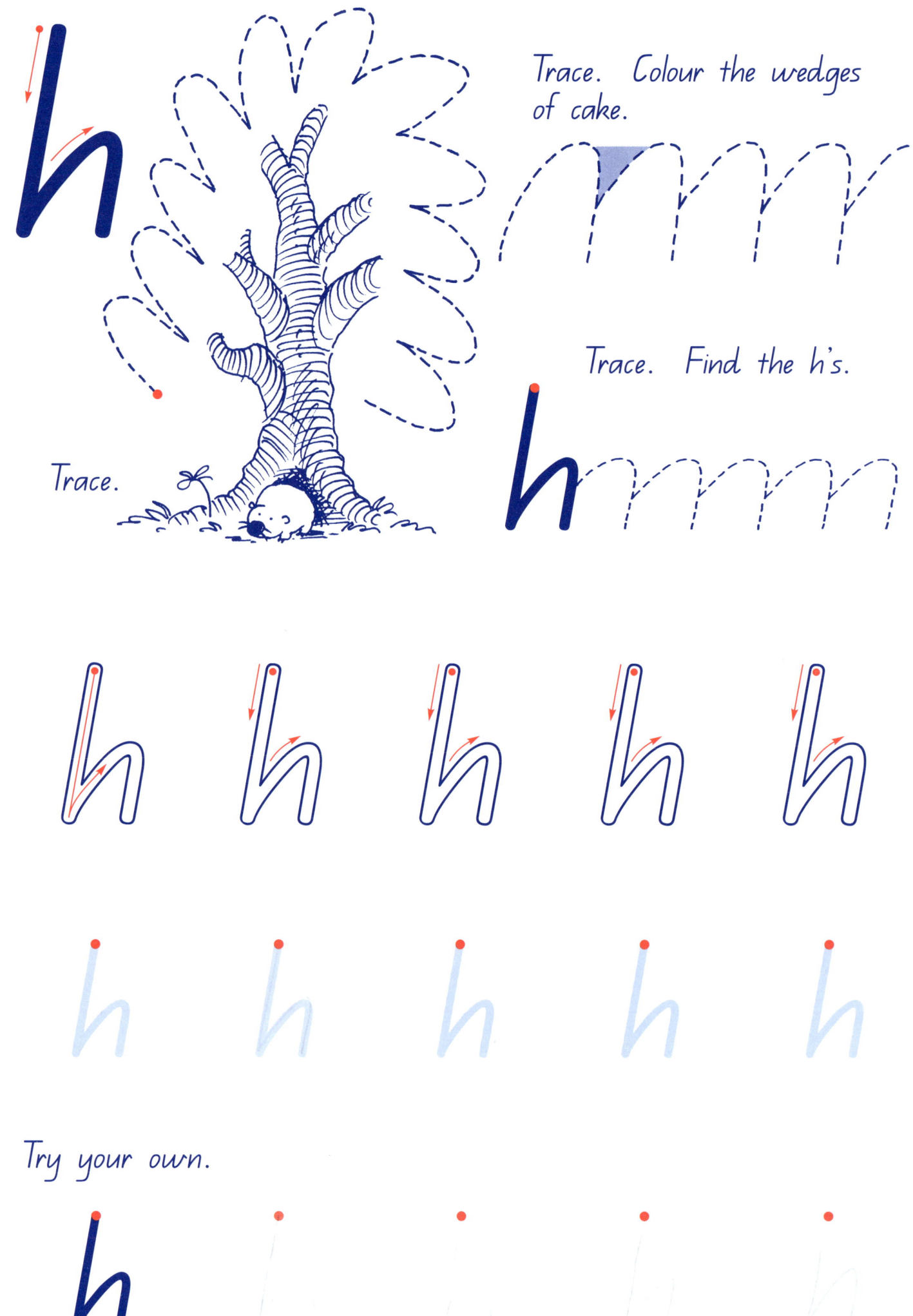

Try your own.

24

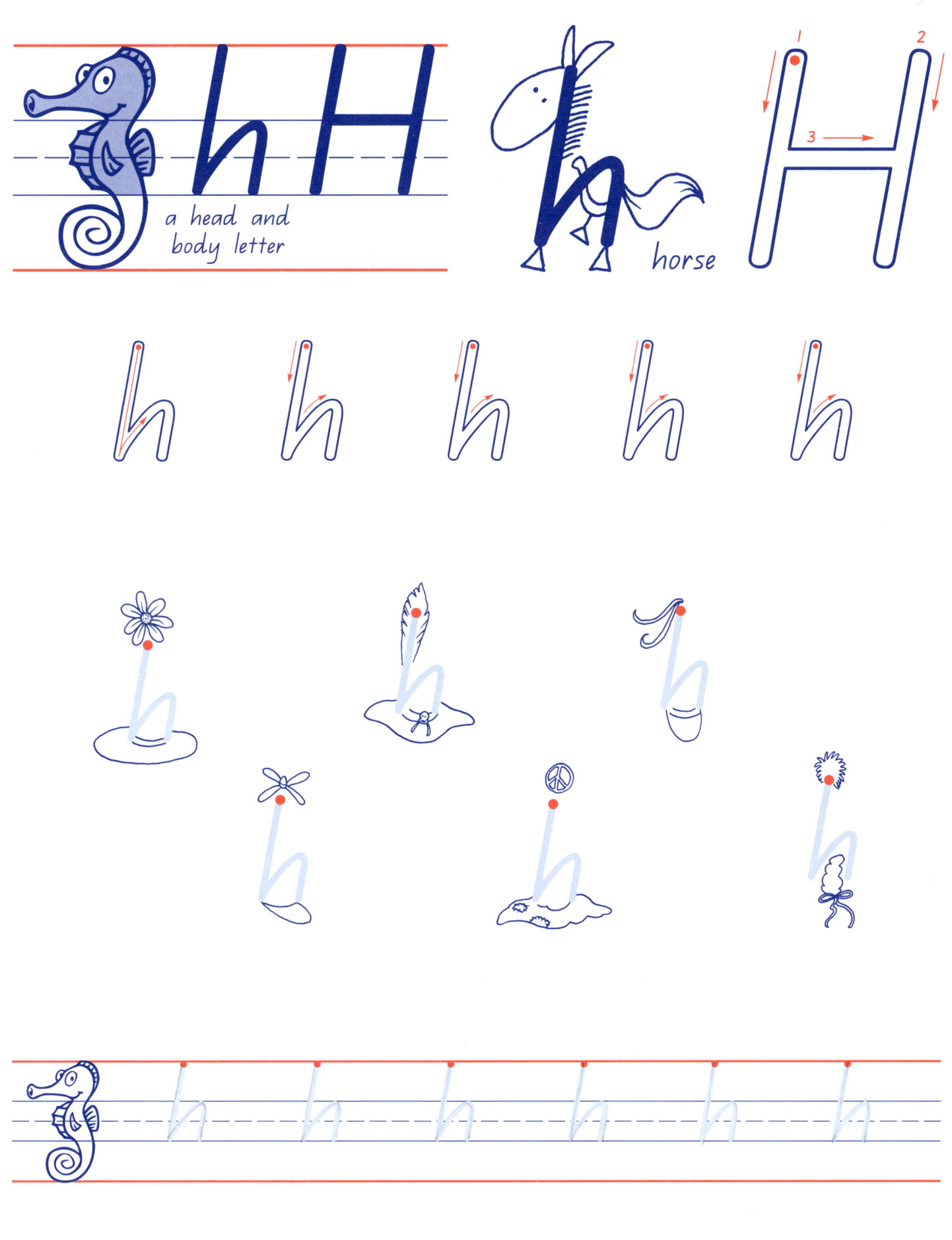

a head and
body letter

horse

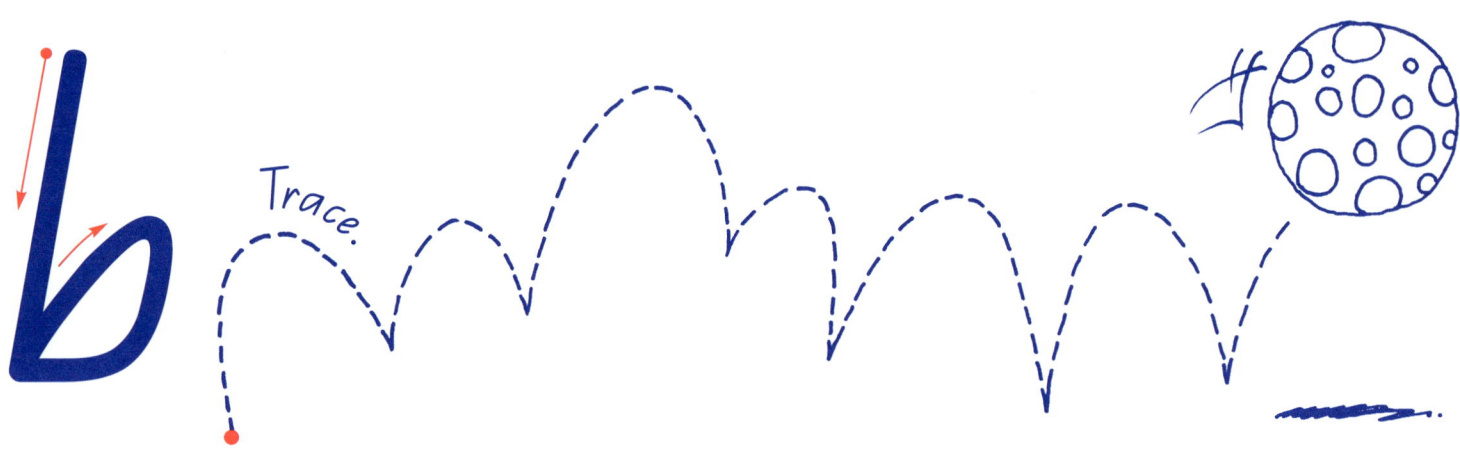

Trace.

Use a crayon to trace the hops.

Trace. Find the b's.

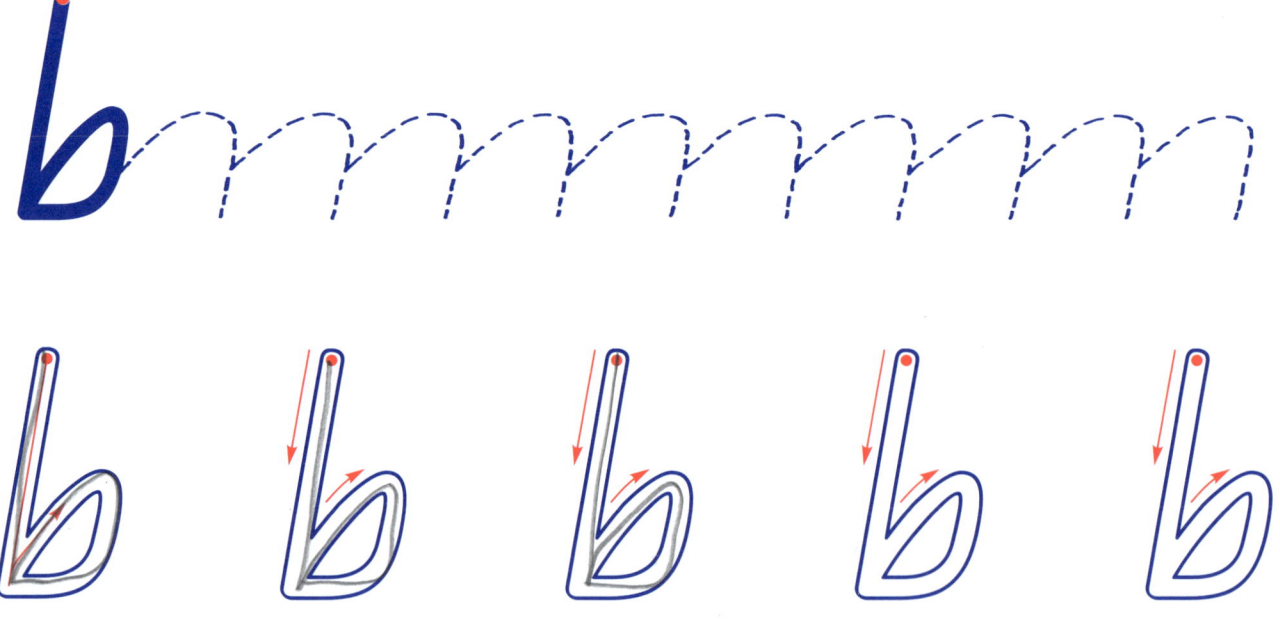

Try your own.

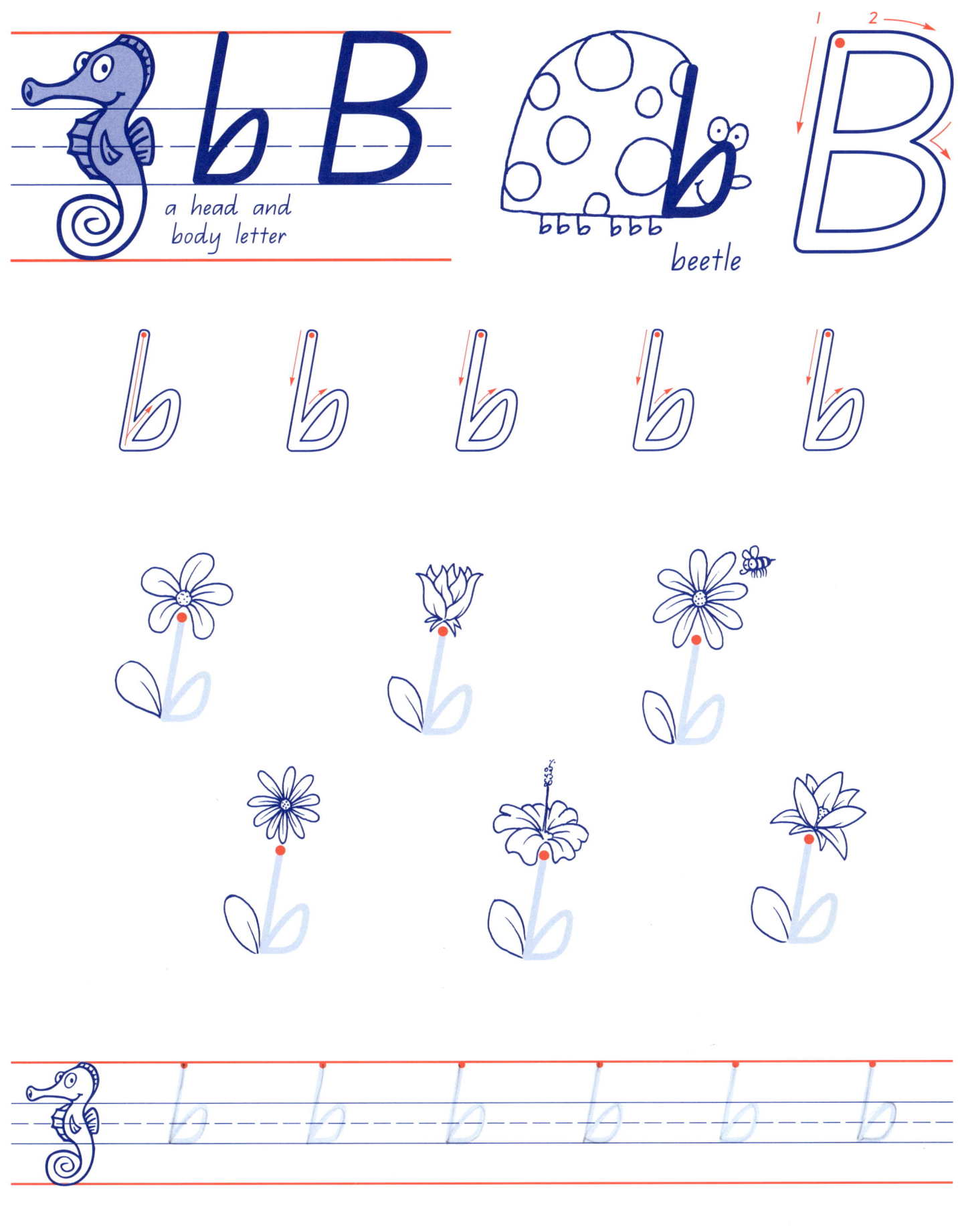

a head and
body letter

beetle

bbb bbb

Trace.

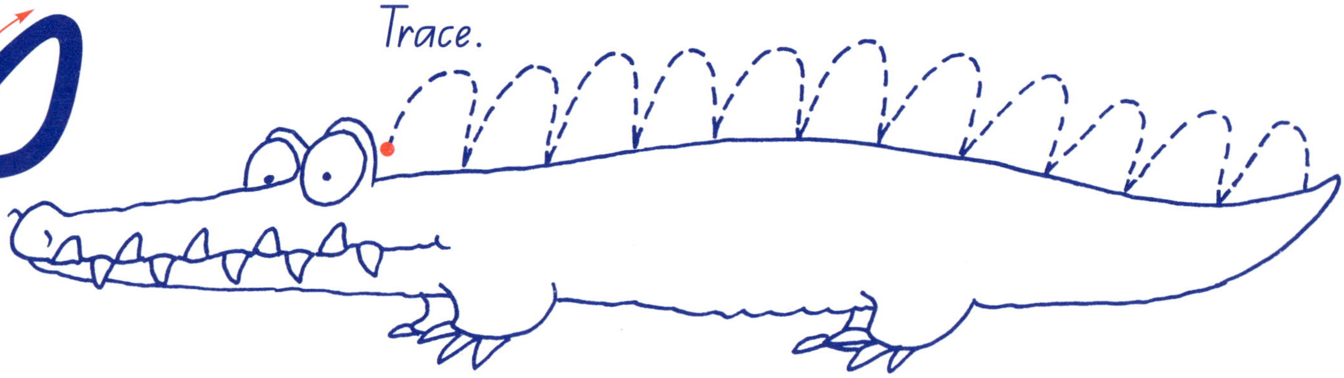

Track.

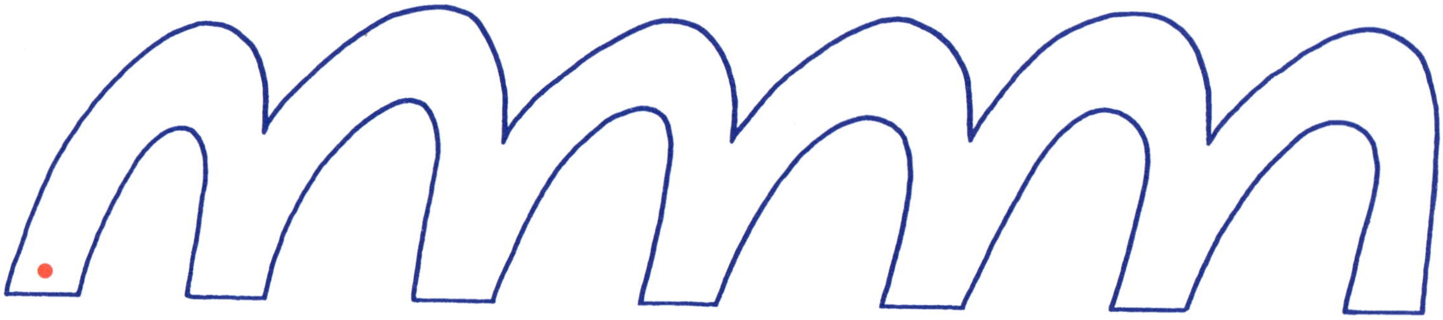

Trace.   Find the p's.

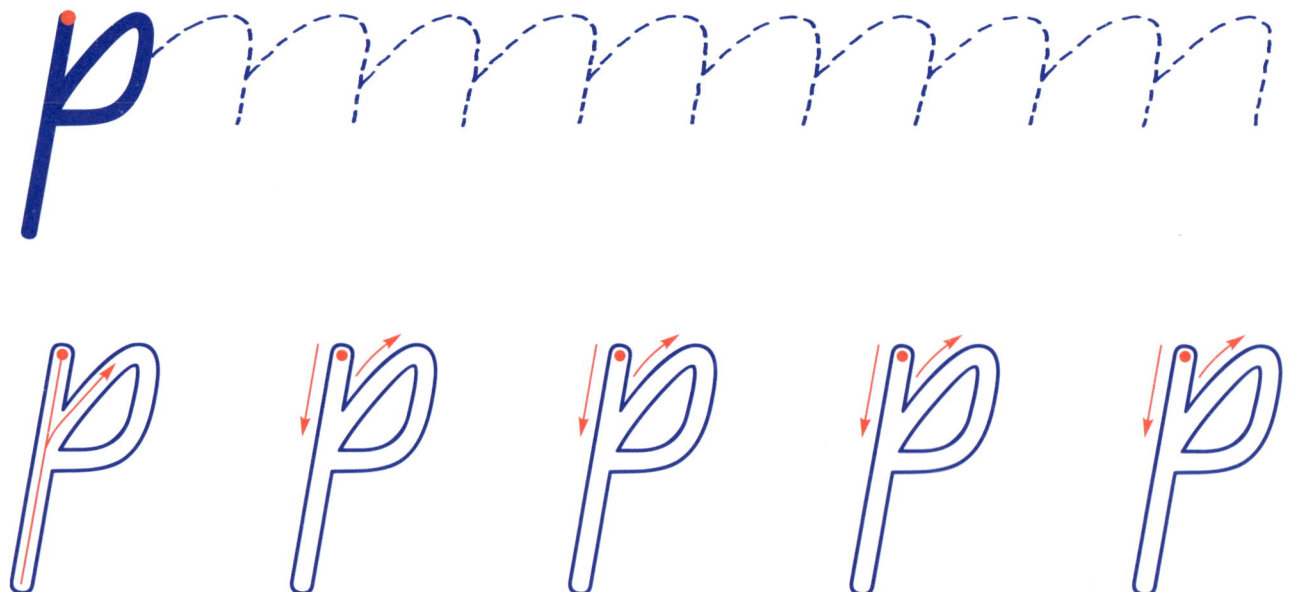

Try your own.

28

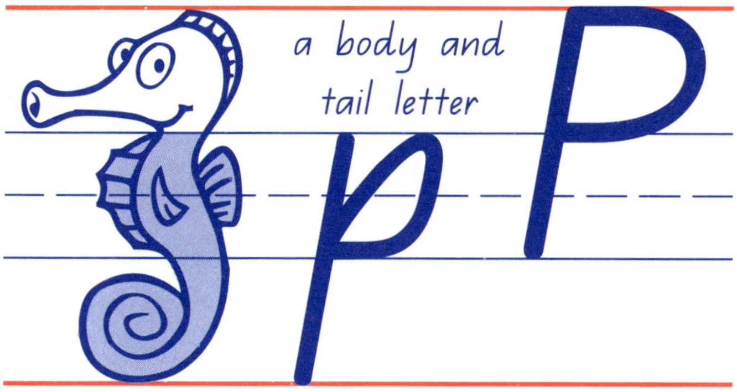

a body and
tail letter

p P

penguin

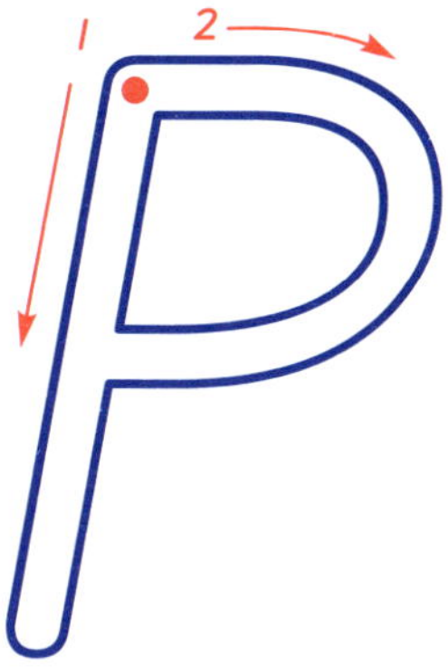

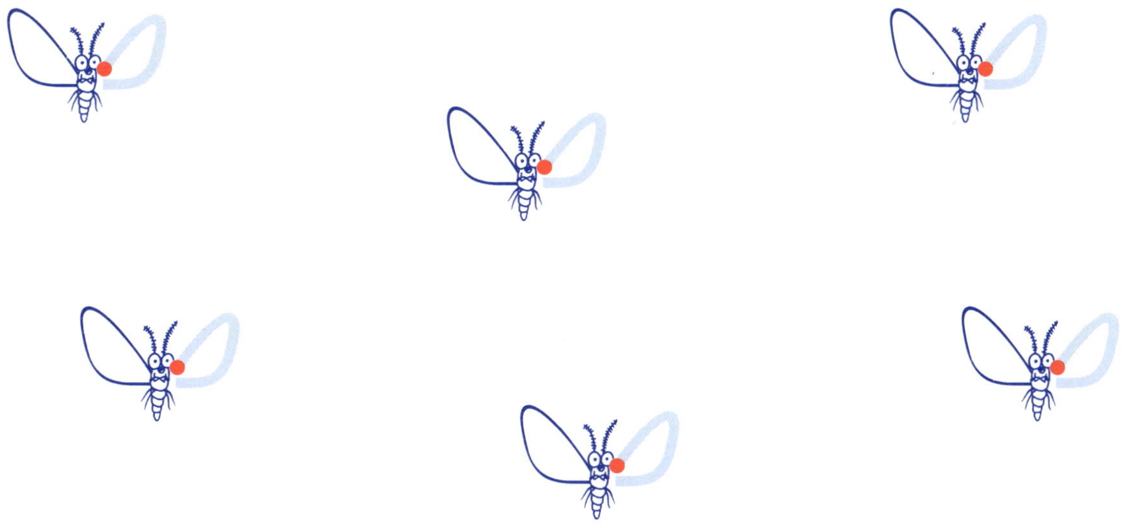

P

p p p p p

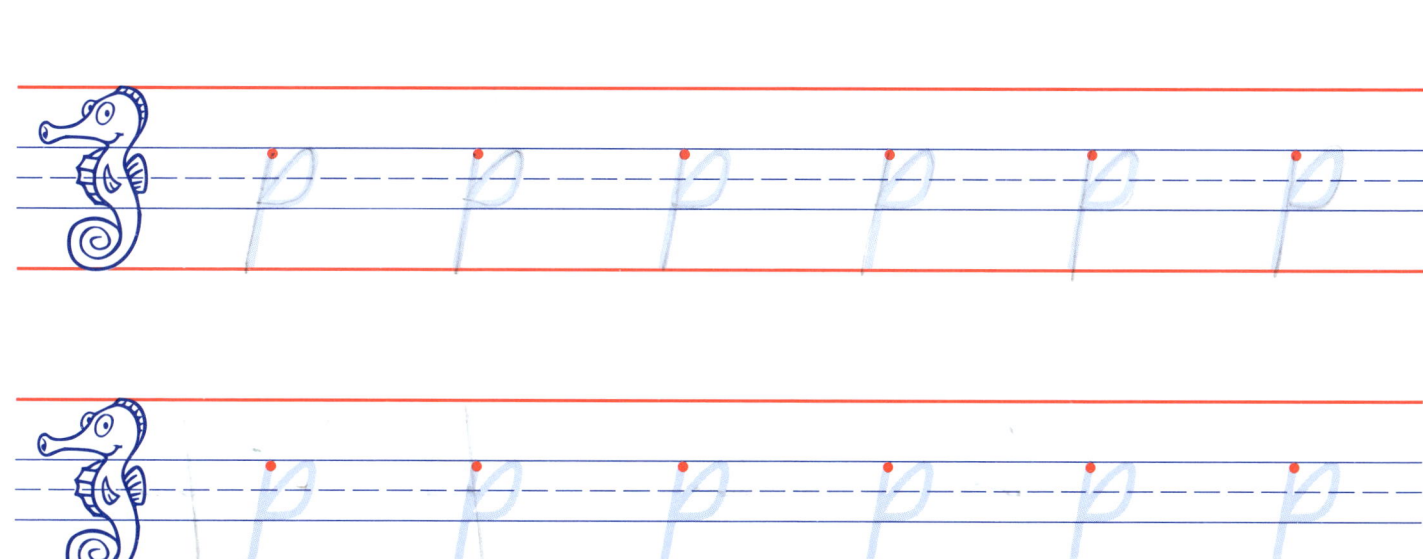

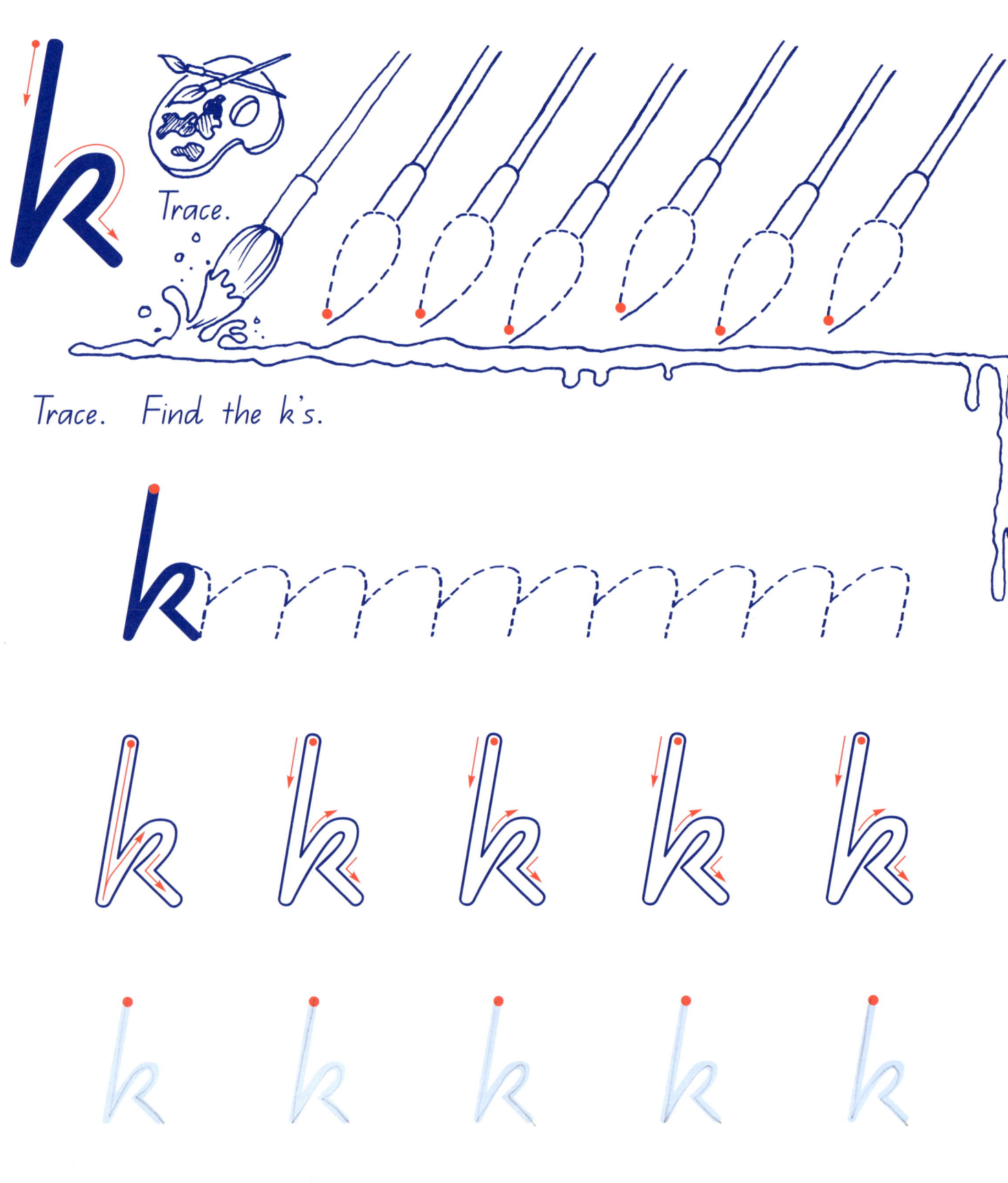

Trace.

Trace. Find the k's.

Try your own.

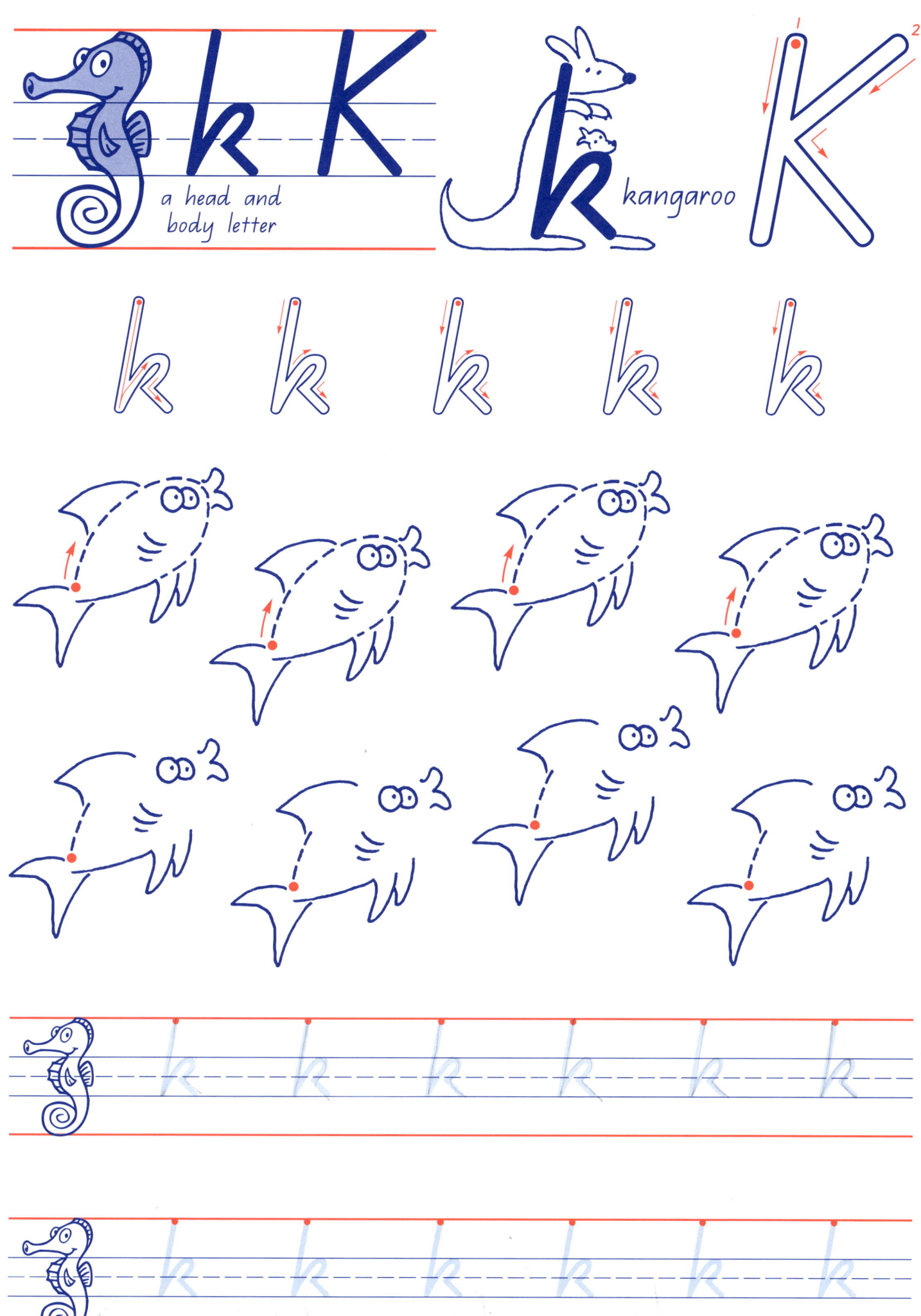

kK

a head and
body letter

kangaroo

Trace.

Trace the waves with 3 different colours.

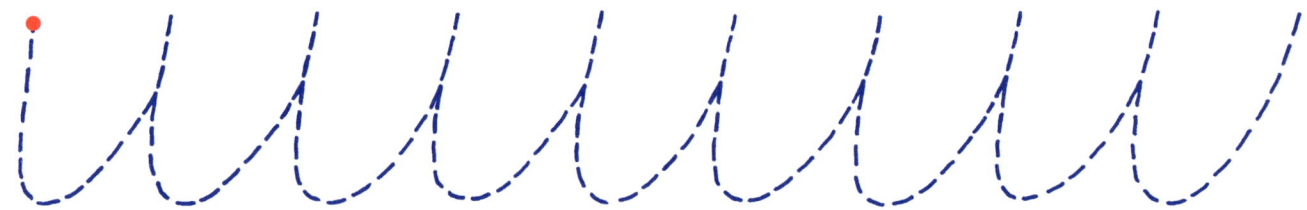

Trace. Find the u's.

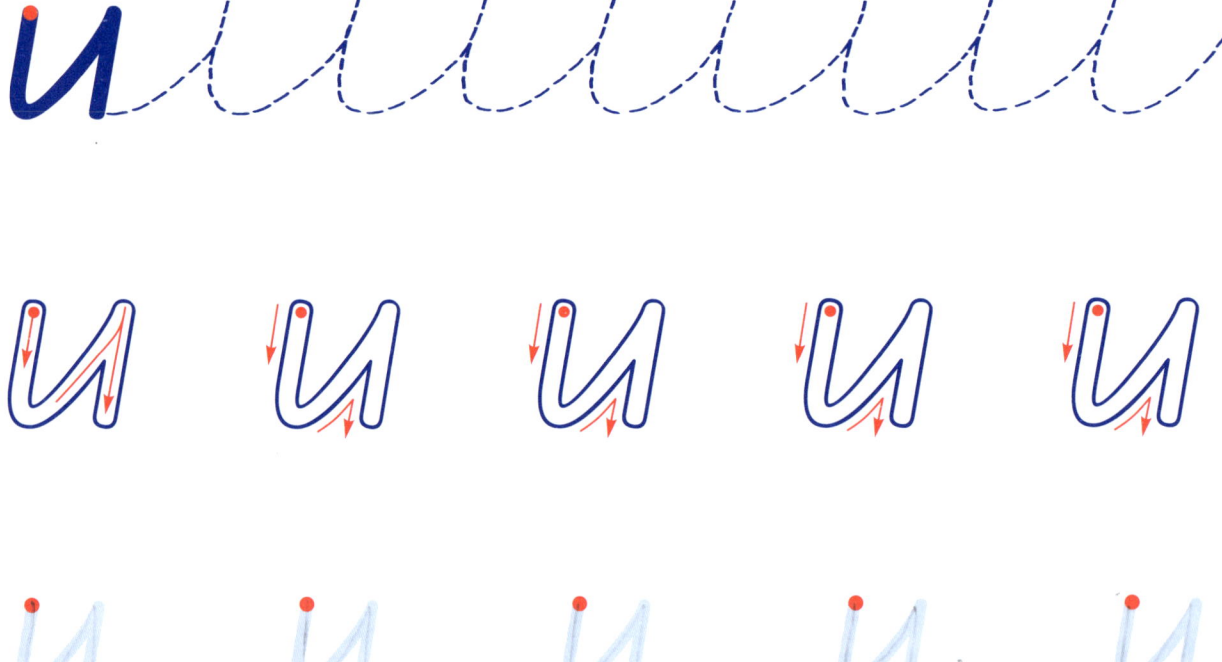

Try your own.

a body letter

underground

33

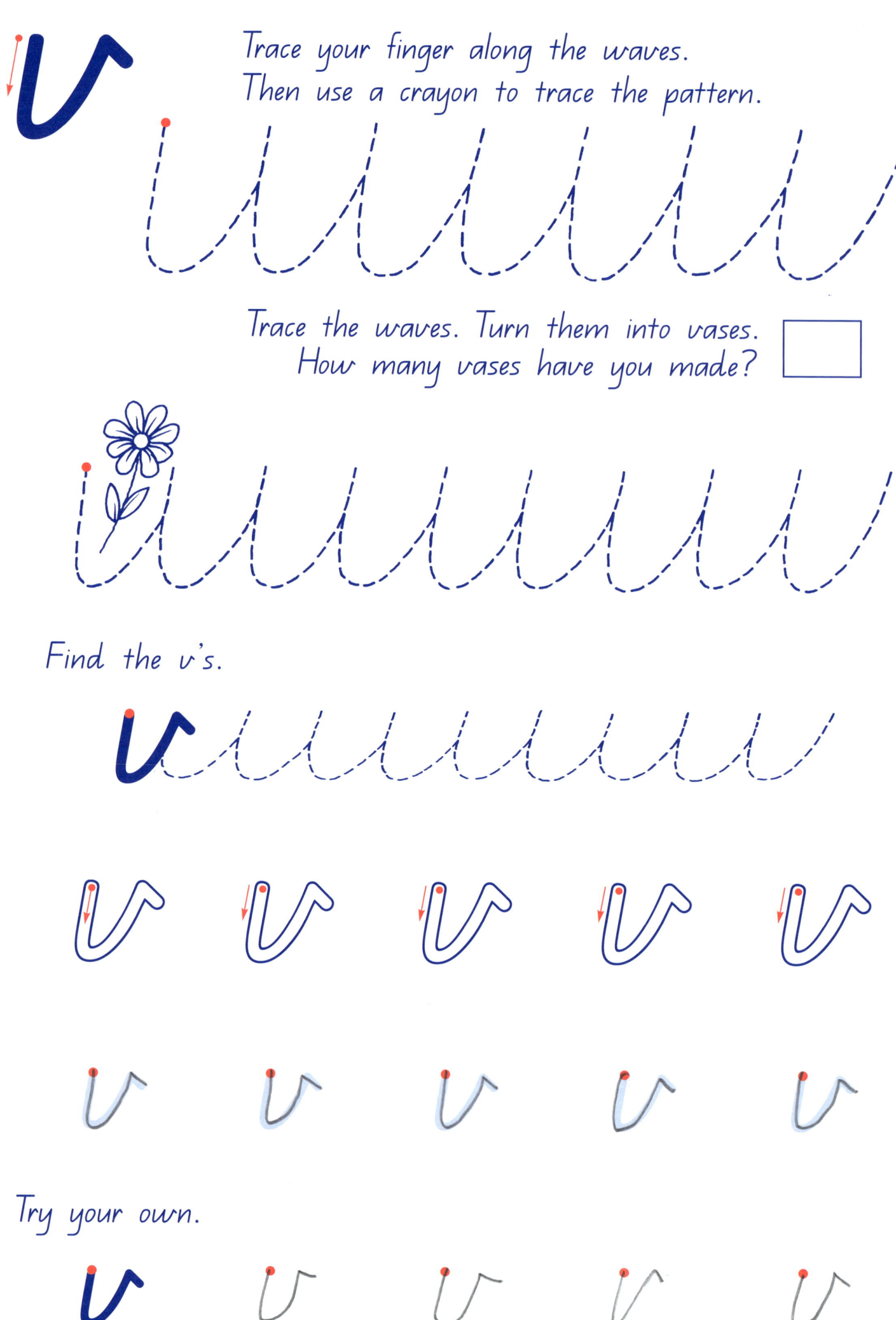

Trace your finger along the waves.
Then use a crayon to trace the pattern.

Trace the waves. Turn them into vases.
How many vases have you made?

Find the v's.

Try your own.

34

a body letter

van

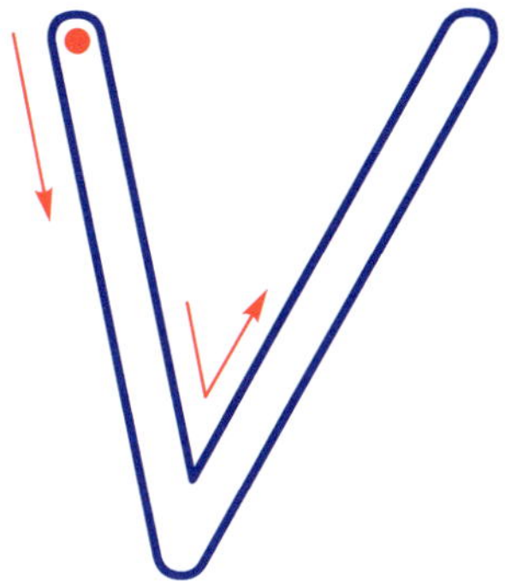

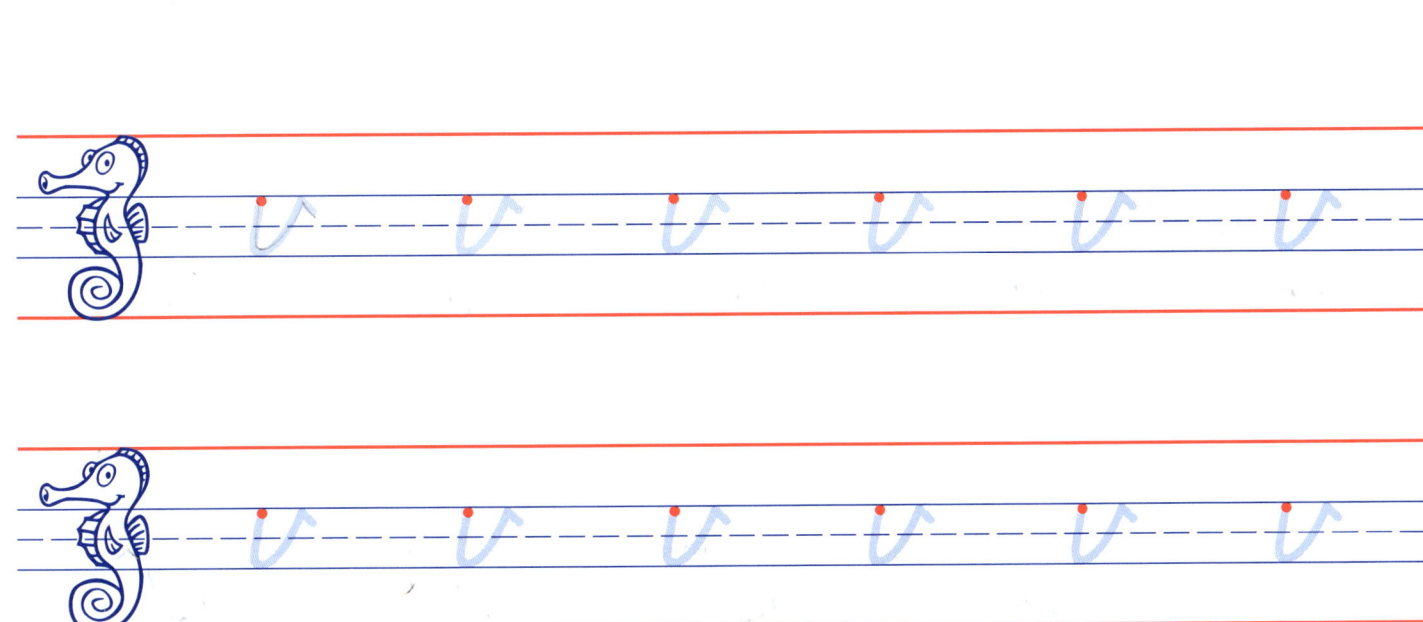

Trace.

Trace.   Colour the wedges of cake.

Find the w's.

Try your own.

a body letter

worm

y Trace.

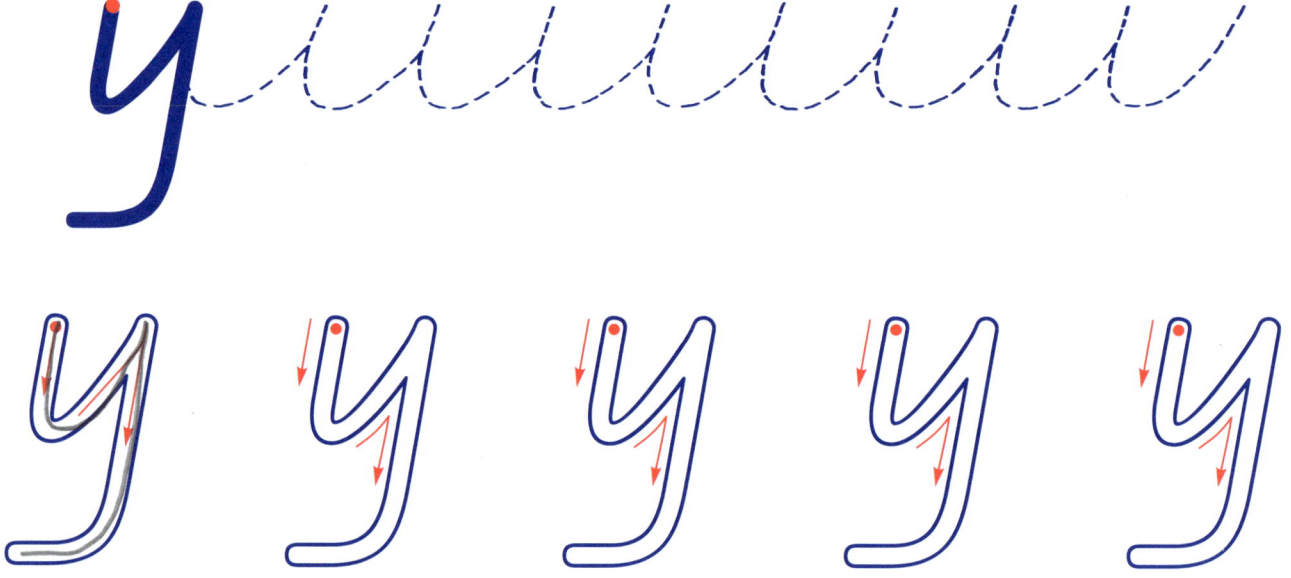

Track.

Trace. Find the y's.

Try your own.

38

a body and tail letter

y Y

yacht

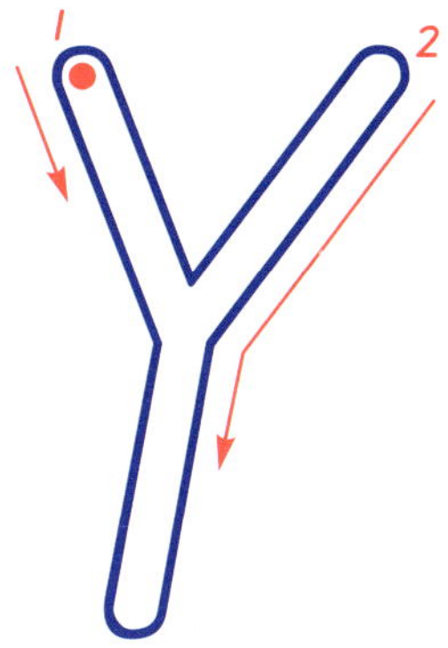

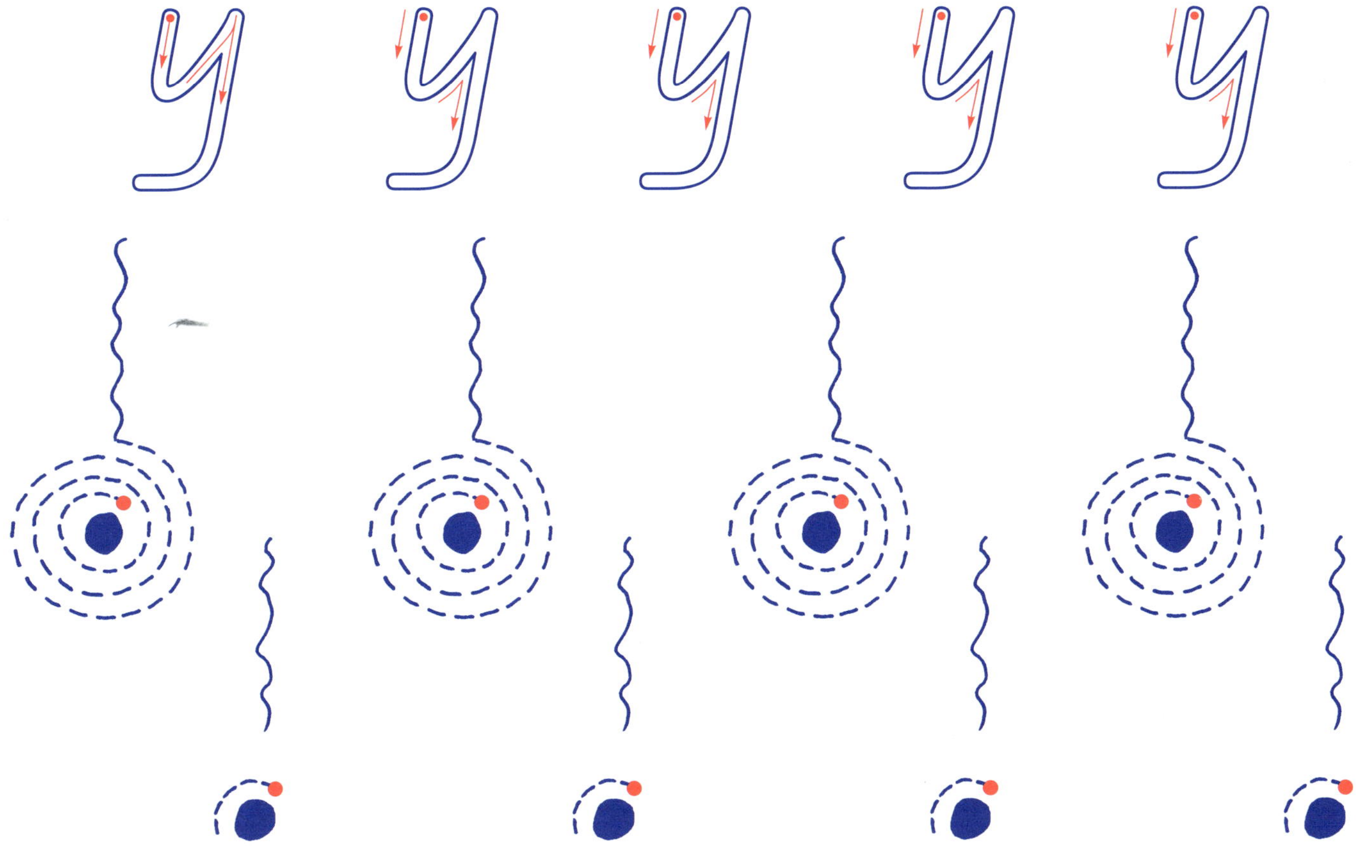

Y

y y y y y

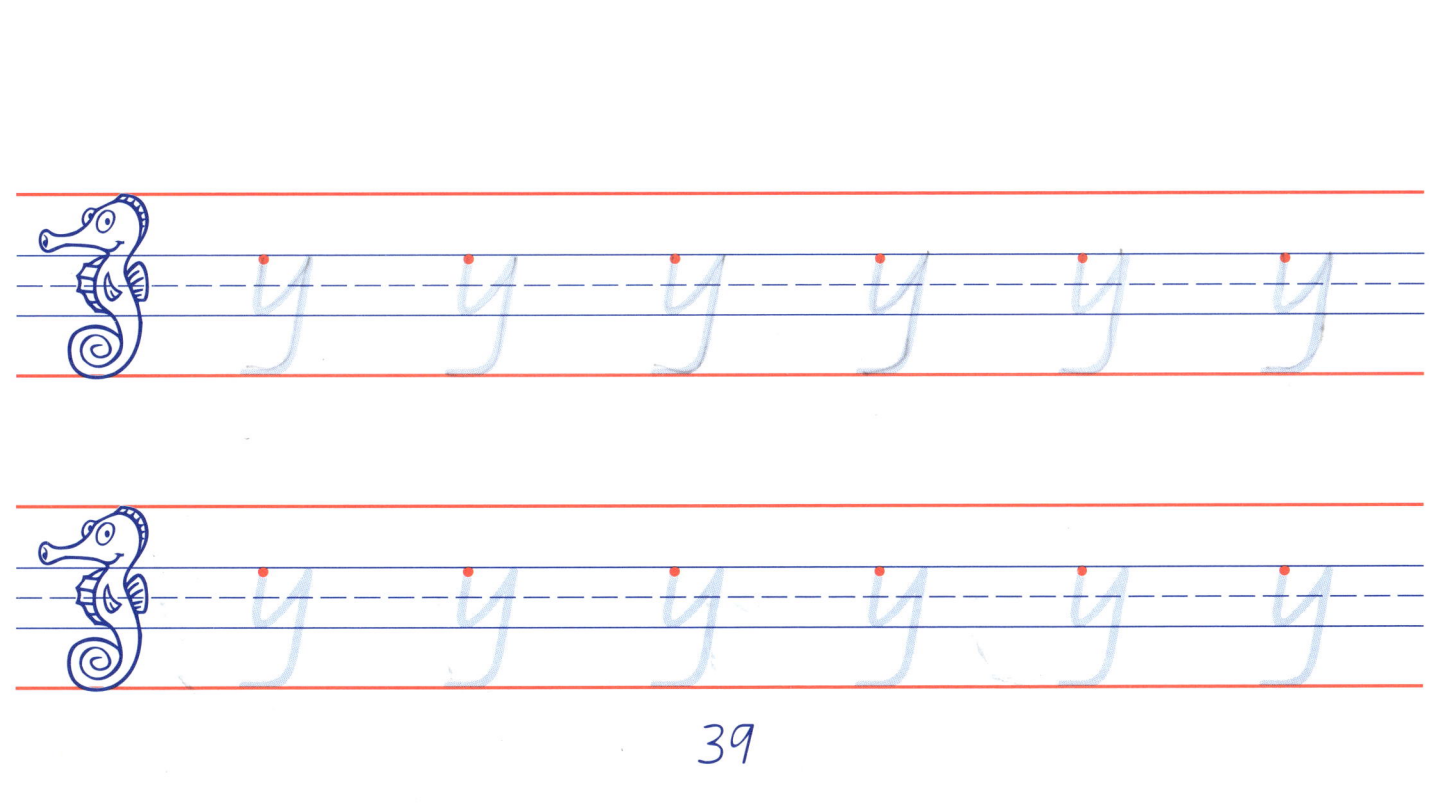

a Trace.

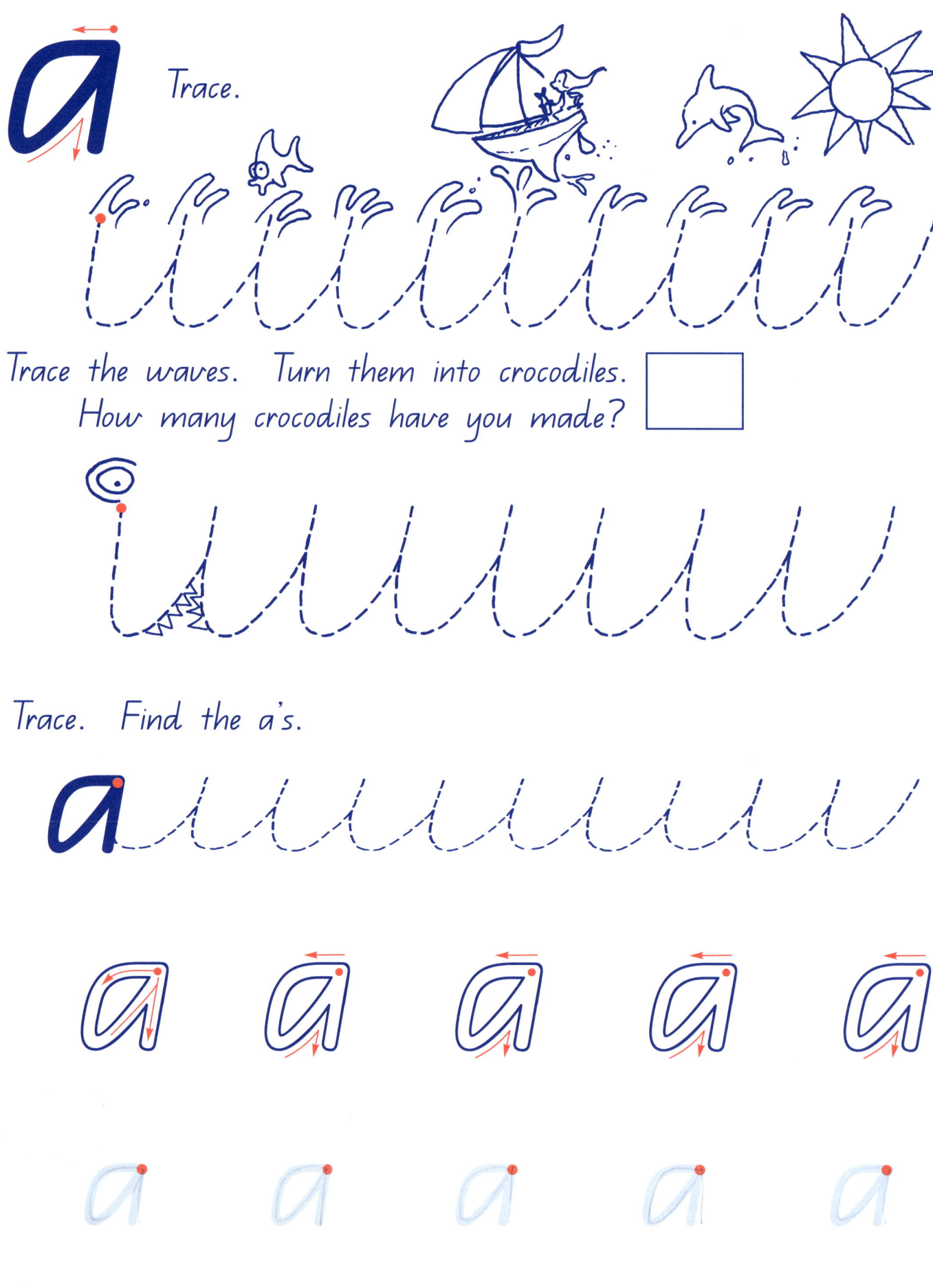

Trace the waves. Turn them into crocodiles.
How many crocodiles have you made?

Trace. Find the a's.

Try your own.

 a body letter

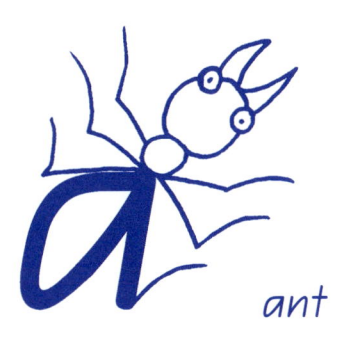 ant

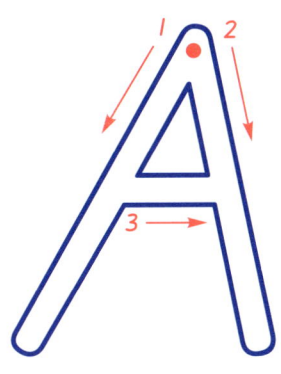

   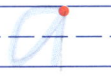   

   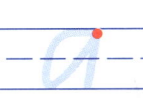 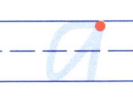 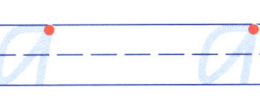

41

Trace.

Use a crayon to trace the waves.

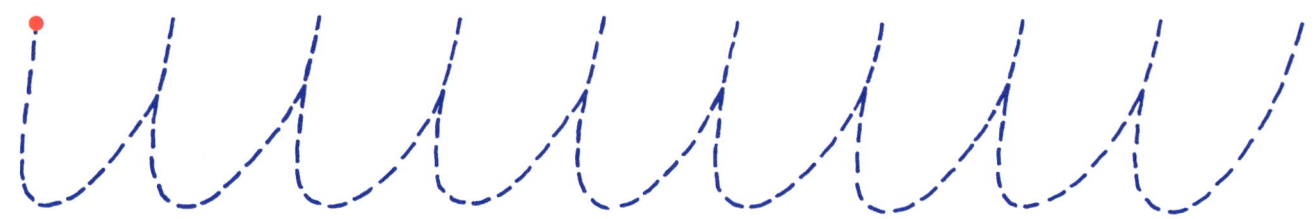

Trace. Find the c's.

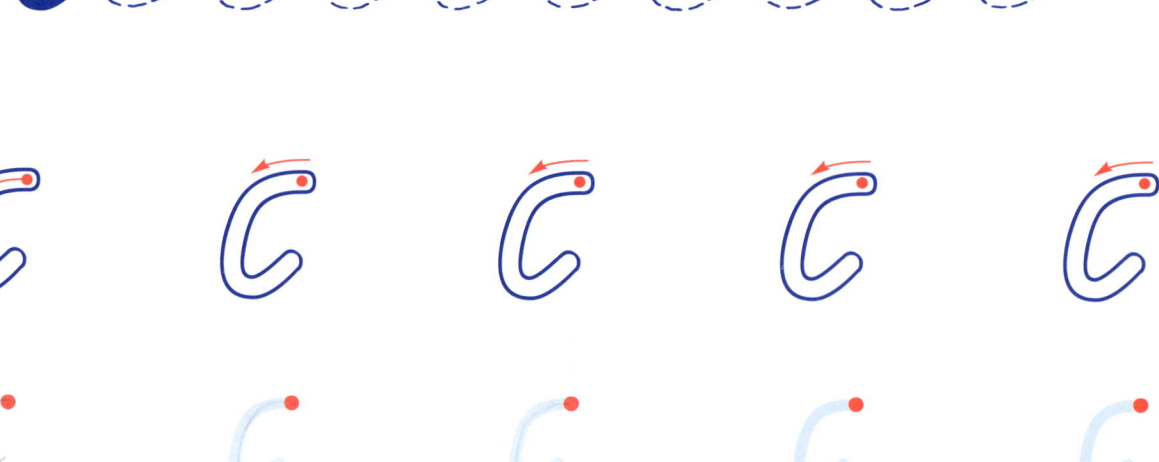

Try your own.

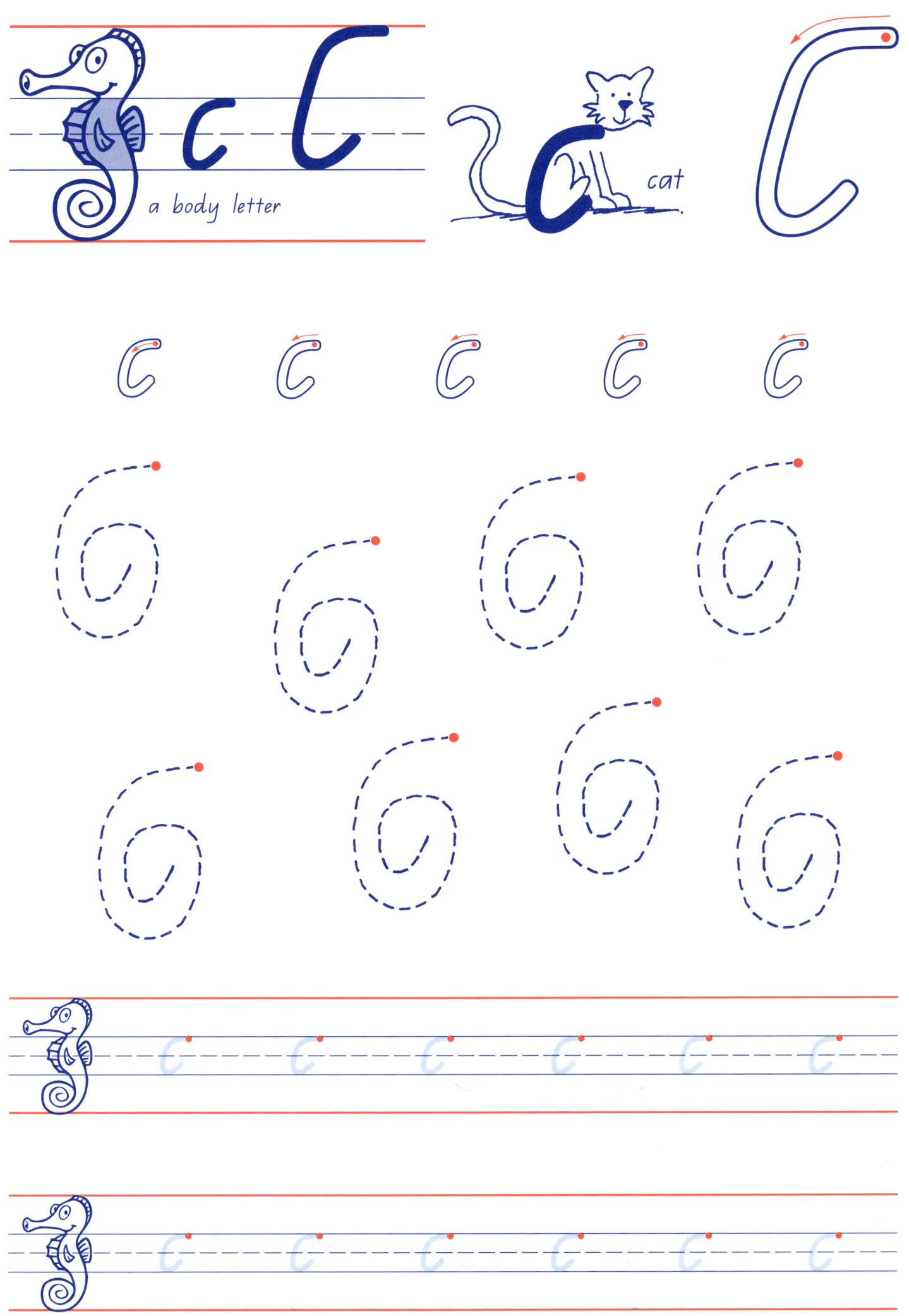

a body letter

cat

O Trace.

Trace. Now turn the waves into your own mice.

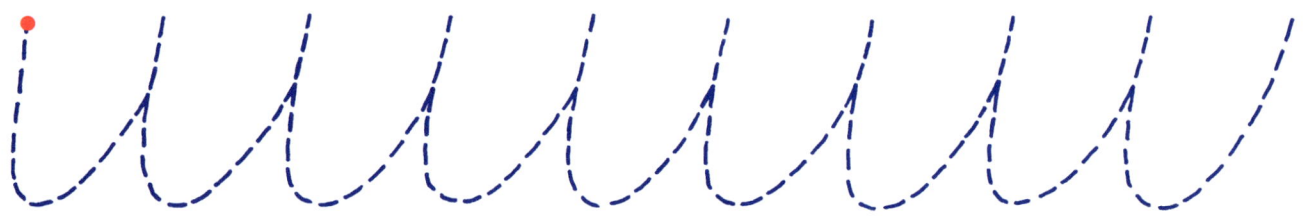

Trace. Find the o's.

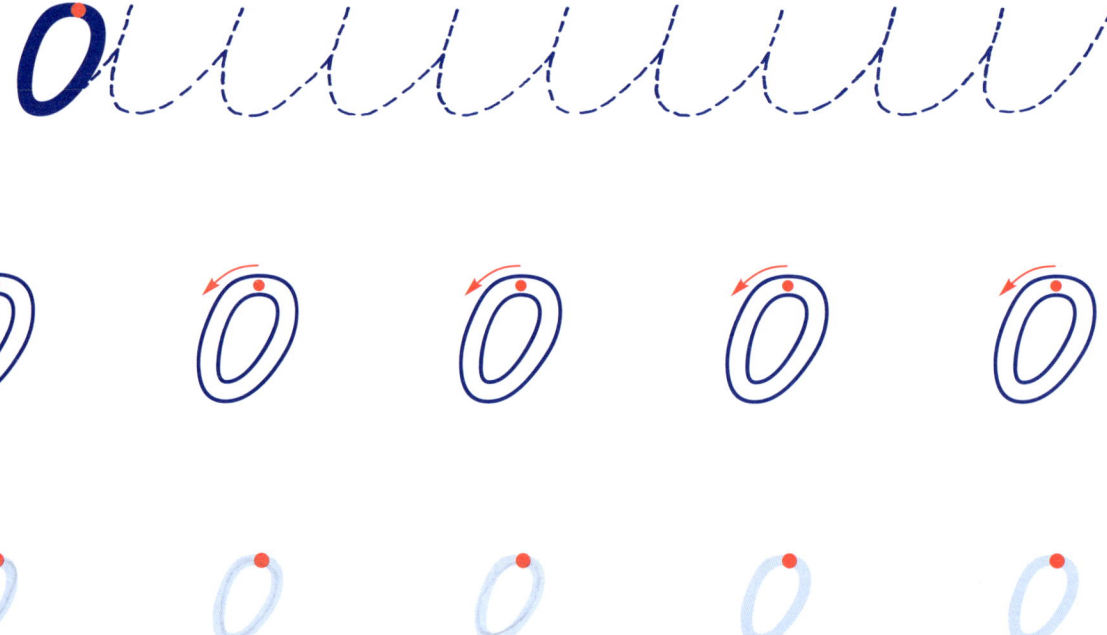

Try your own.

O

a body letter

ostrich

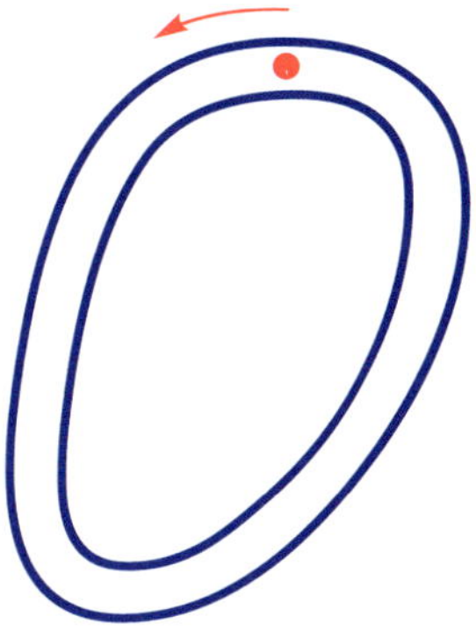

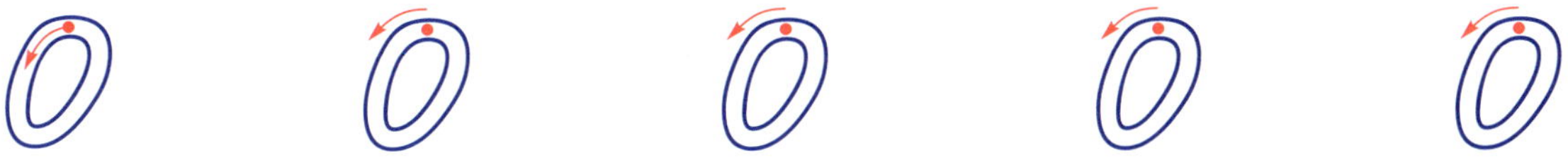

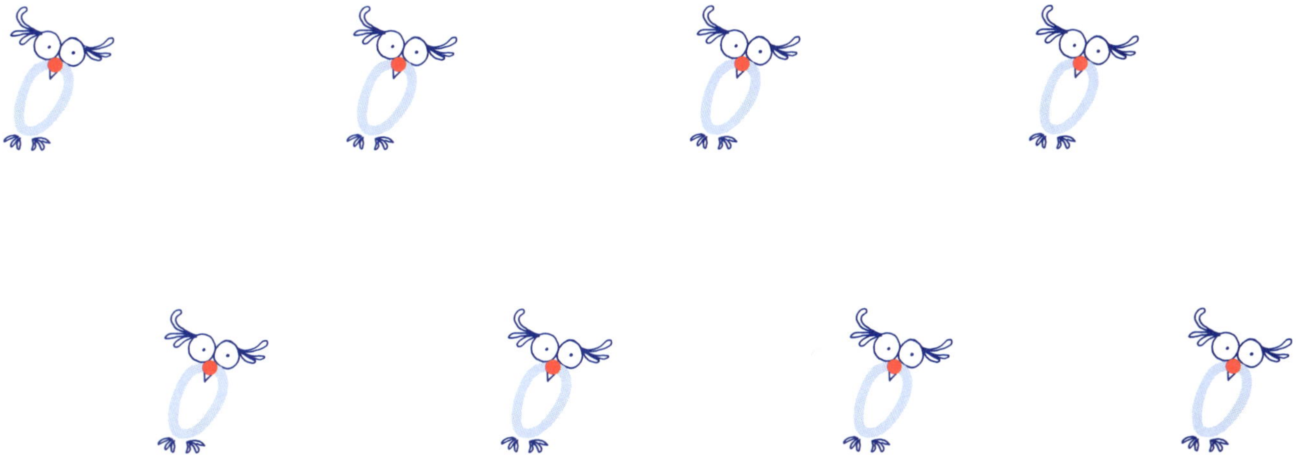

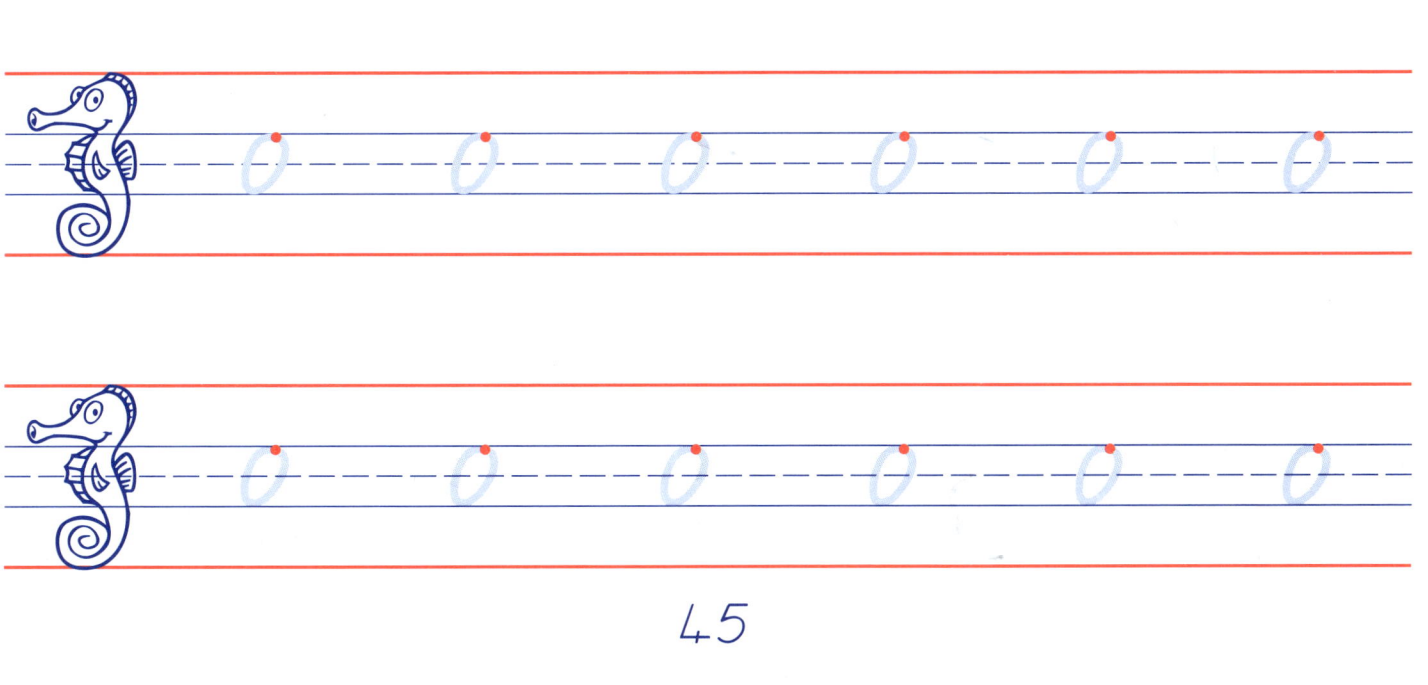

g

Trace.

Trace the waves with your fingers, then use a crayon to trace them.

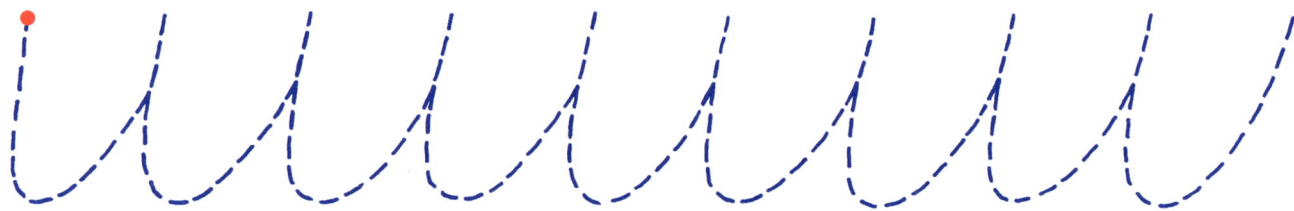

Trace. Find the g's.

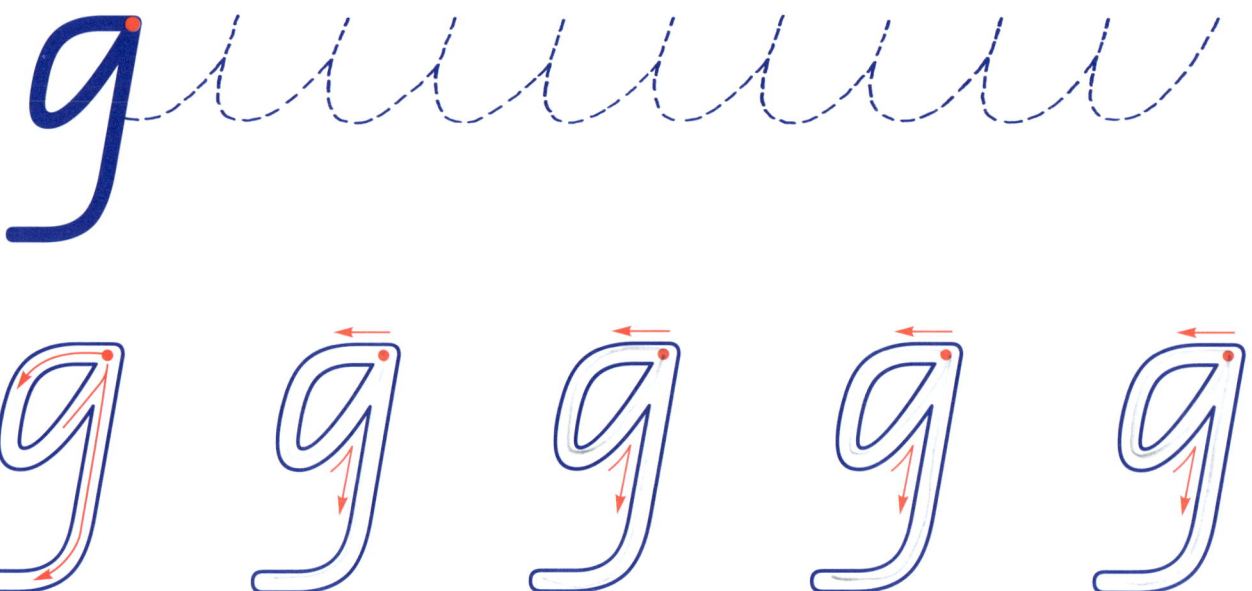

Try your own.

g

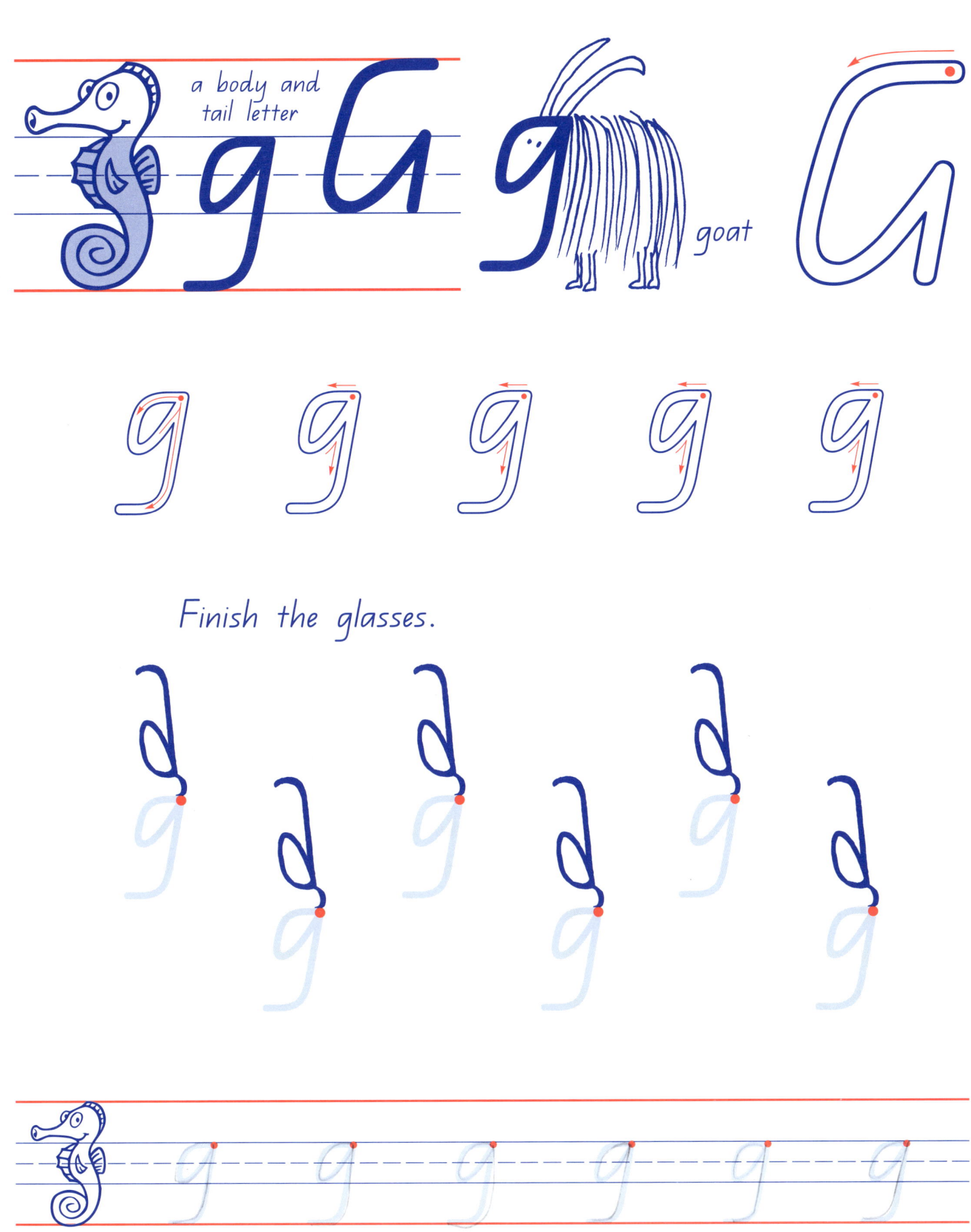

a body and
tail letter

goat

Finish the glasses.

Track.

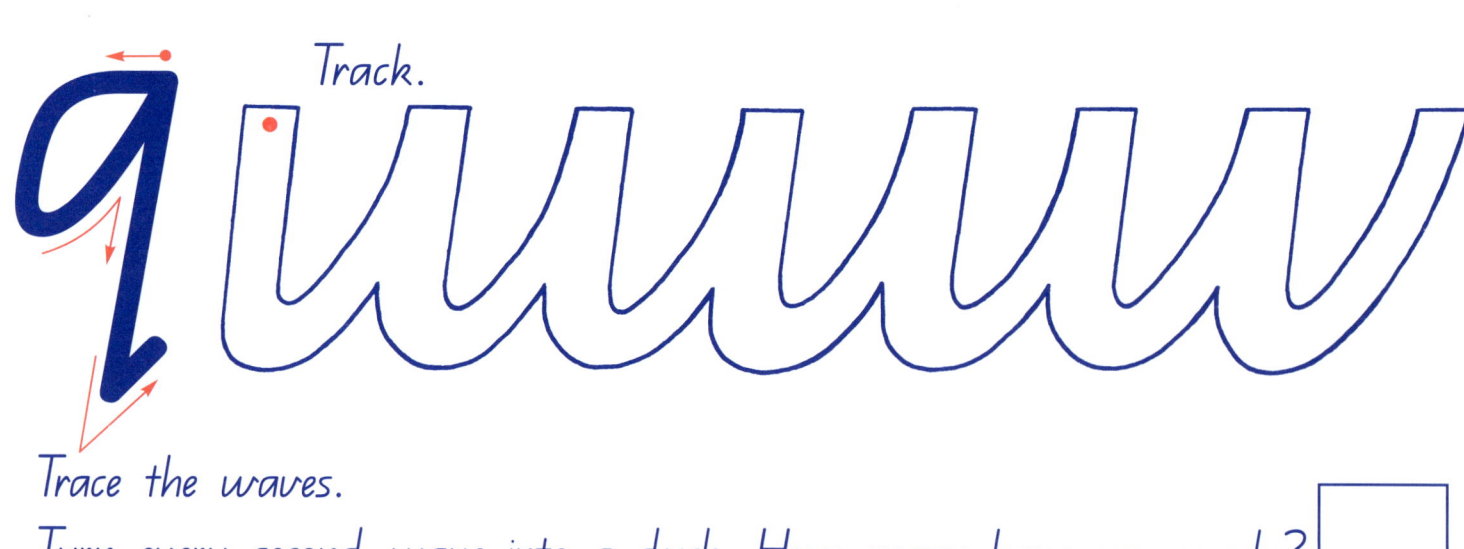

Trace the waves.
Turn every second wave into a duck. How many have you made? ▢

Trace. Find the q's.

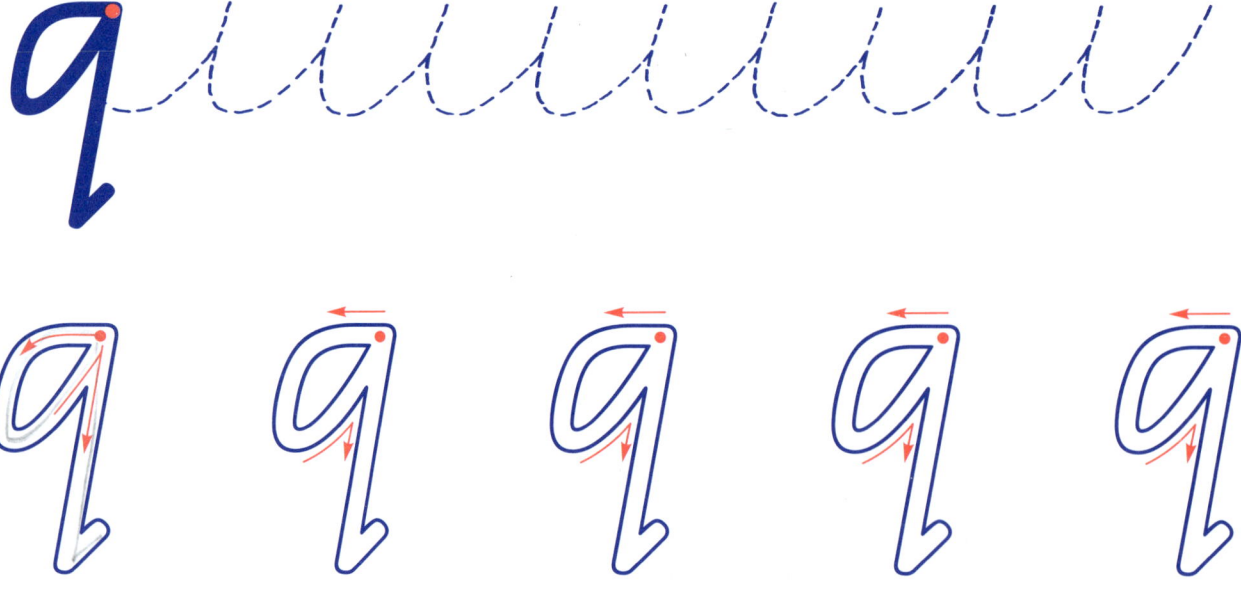

Try your own.

q

a body and
tail letter

q Q

queen

Q

q q q q q

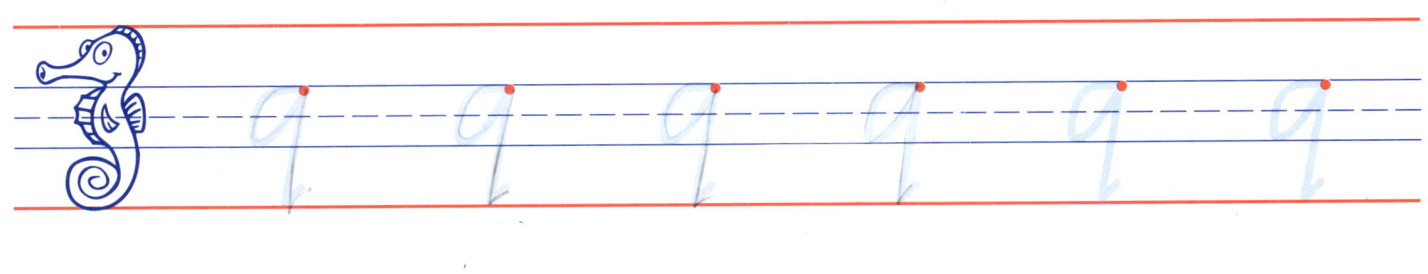

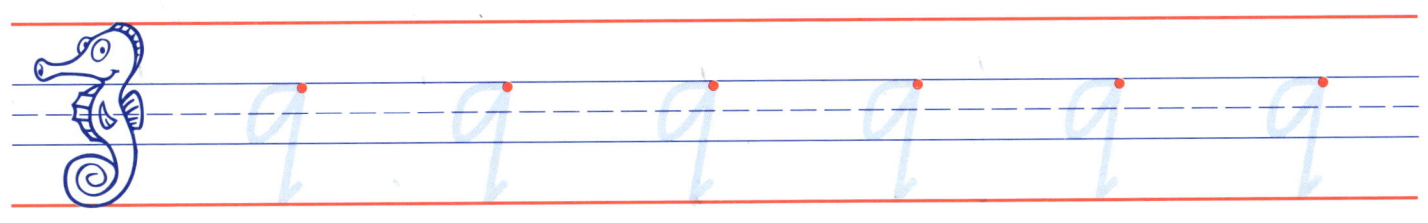

49

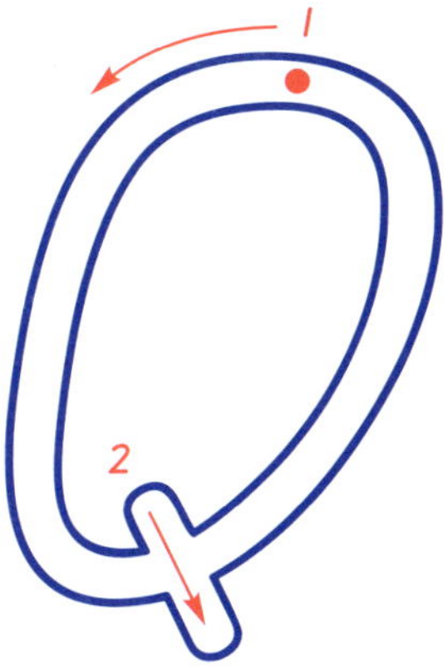

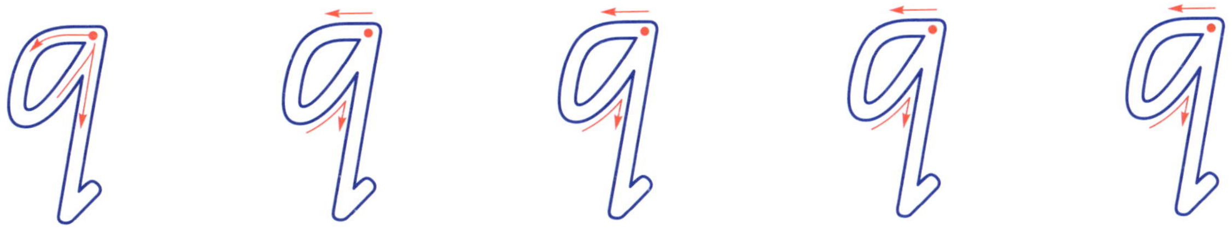

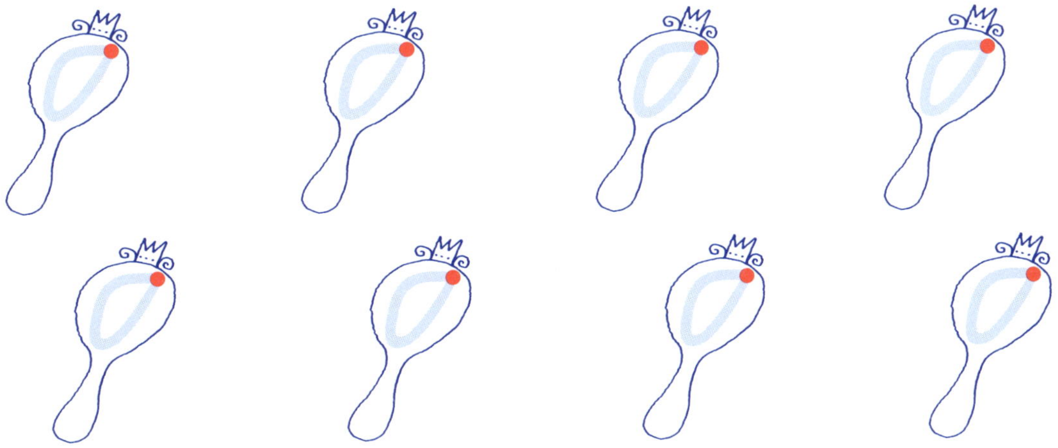

Trace.

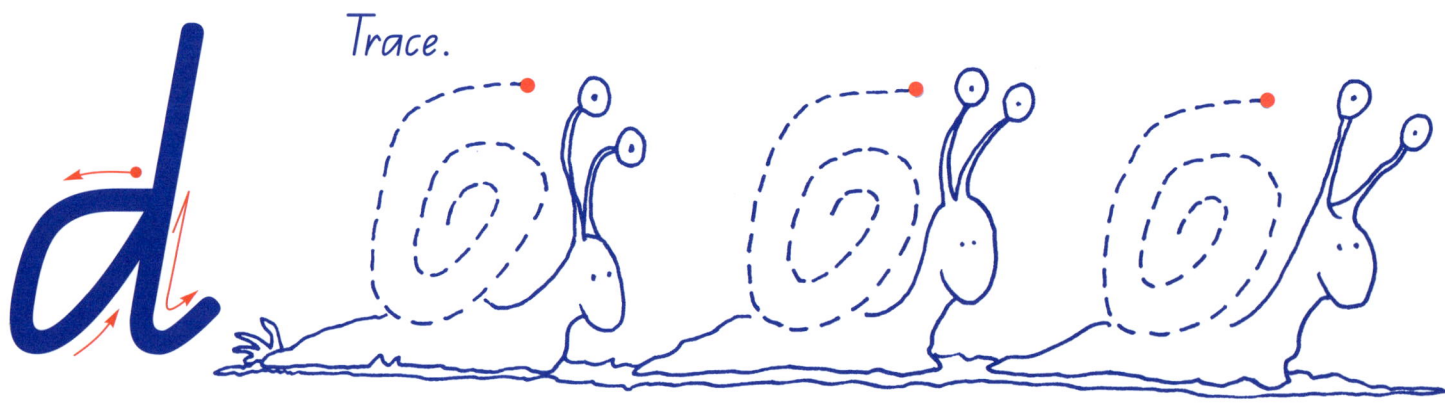

Trace. Turn the waves into faces.

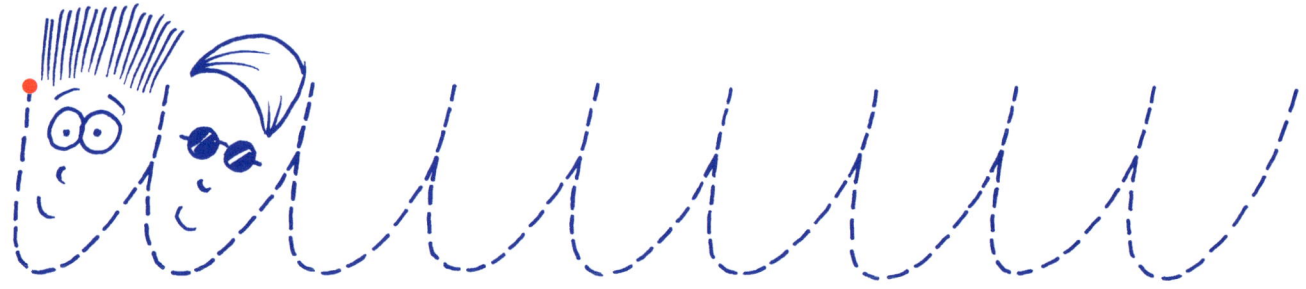

Trace. Find the d's.

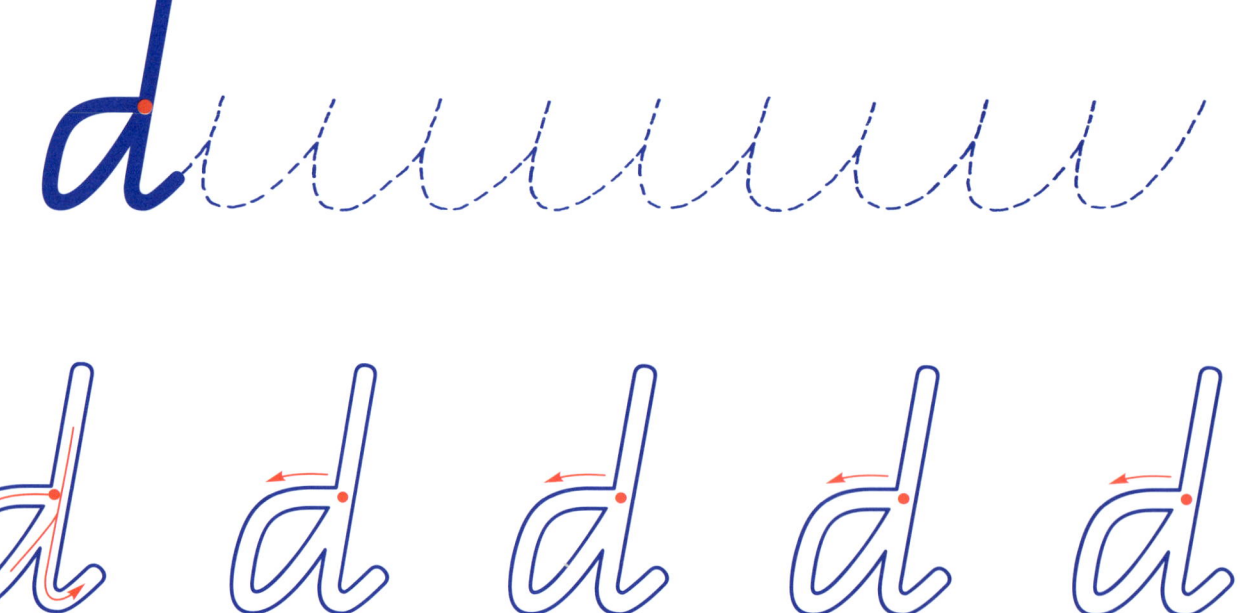

Try your own.

dD

a head and
body letter

dinosaur

1 2

d   d   d   d   d

Finish
the cherries.

d   d   d   d   d   d

d   d   d   d   d   d

51

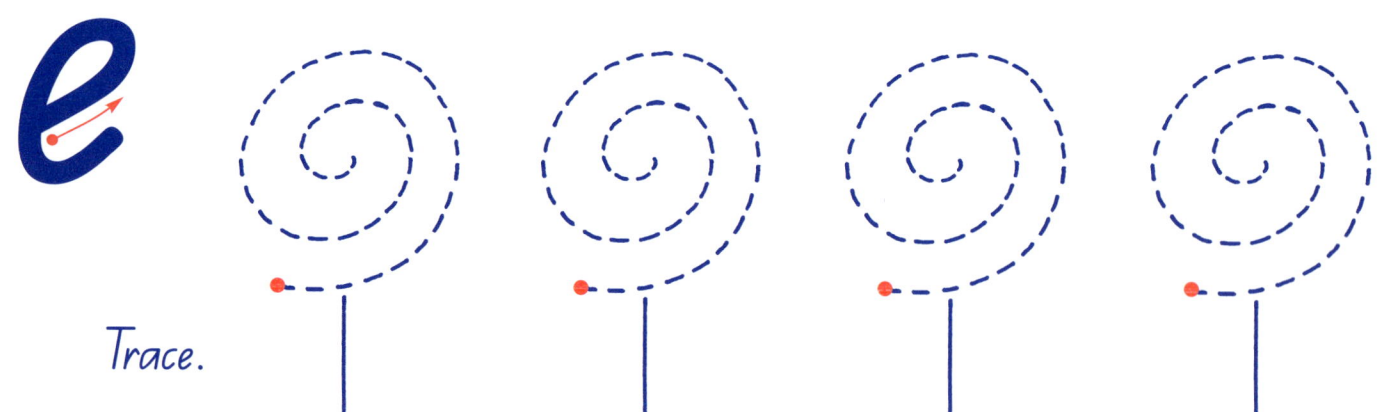

Trace.

Trace. Colour the wedges.

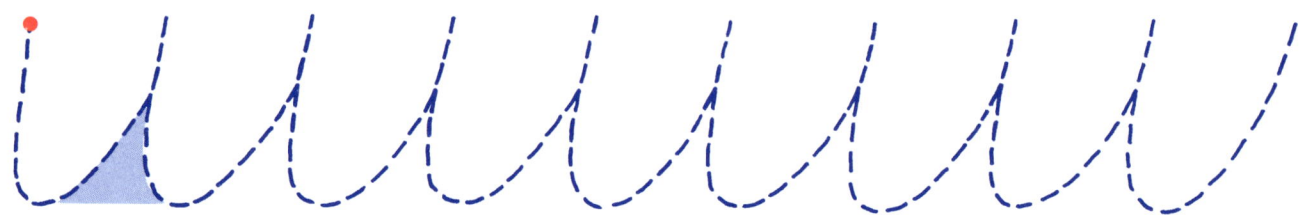

Trace. Find the e's.

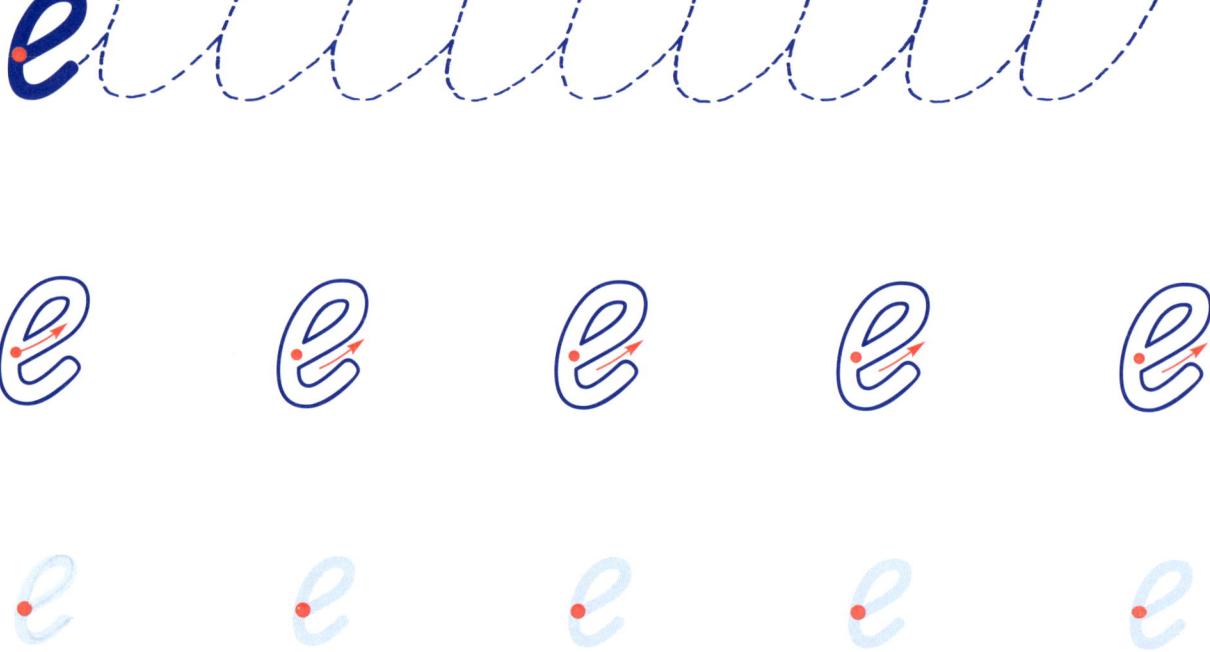

Try your own.

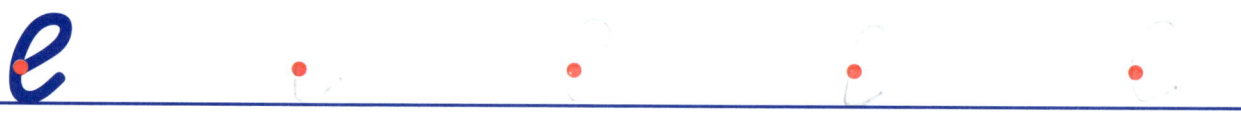

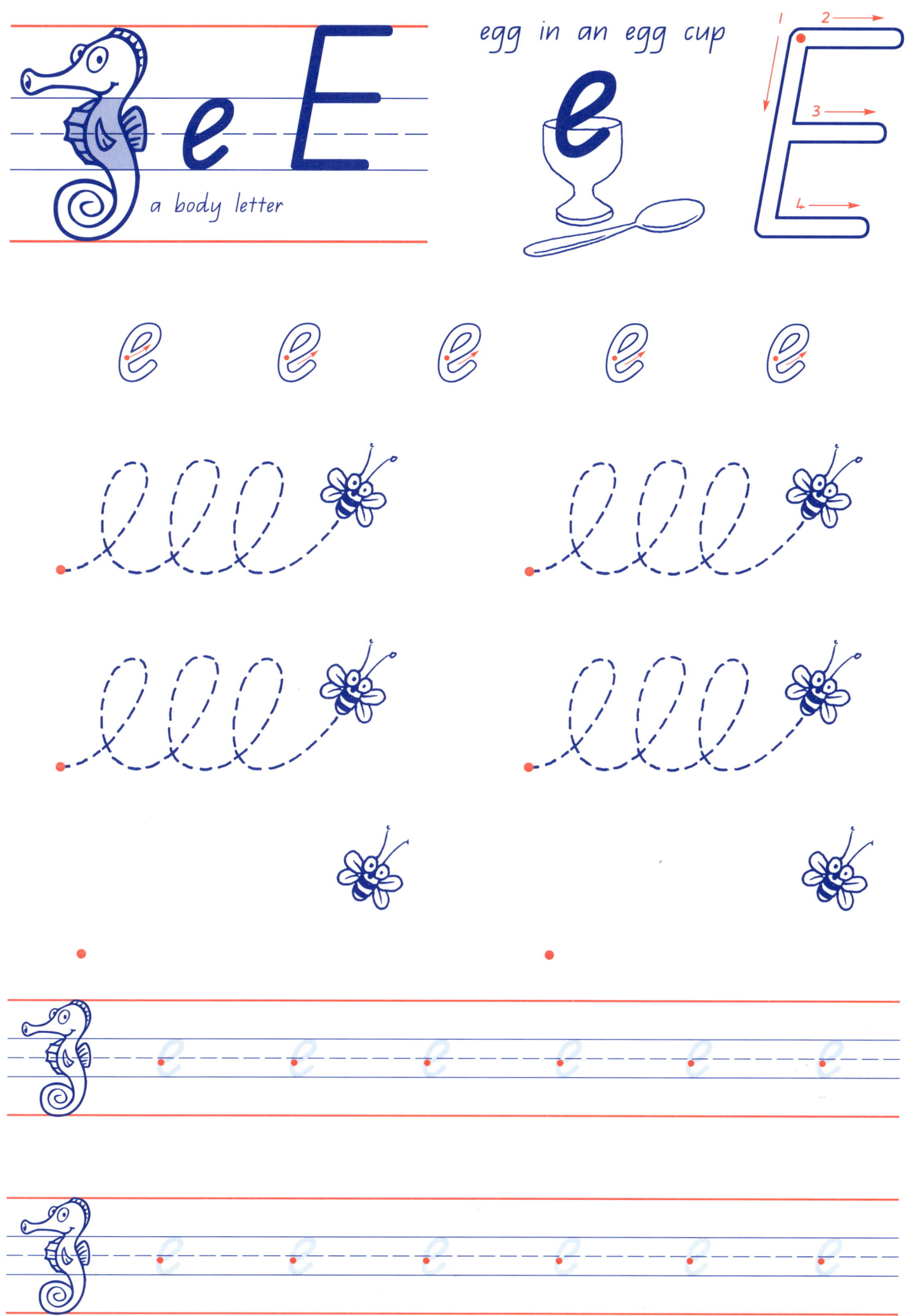

a body letter

egg in an egg cup

S

Trace.

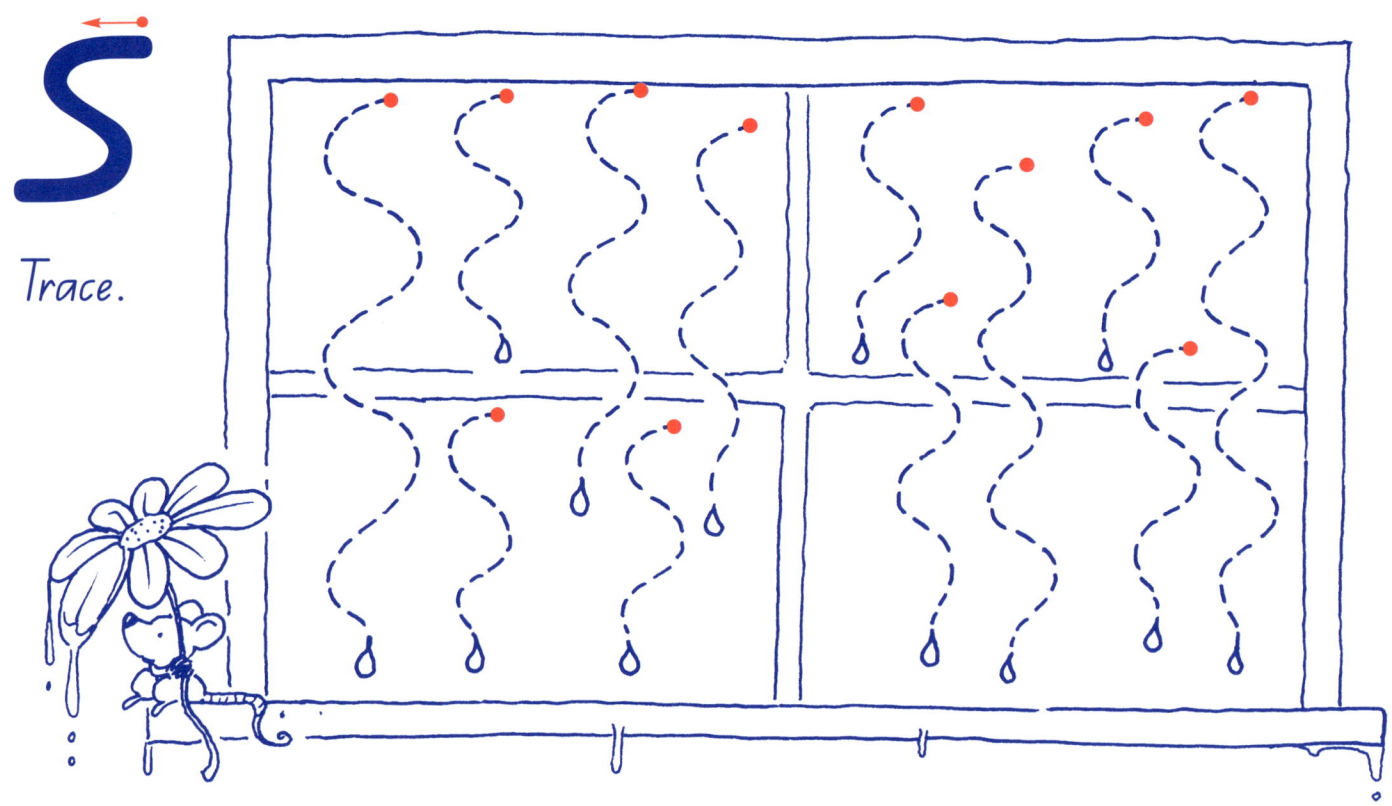

Trace. Find the s's.

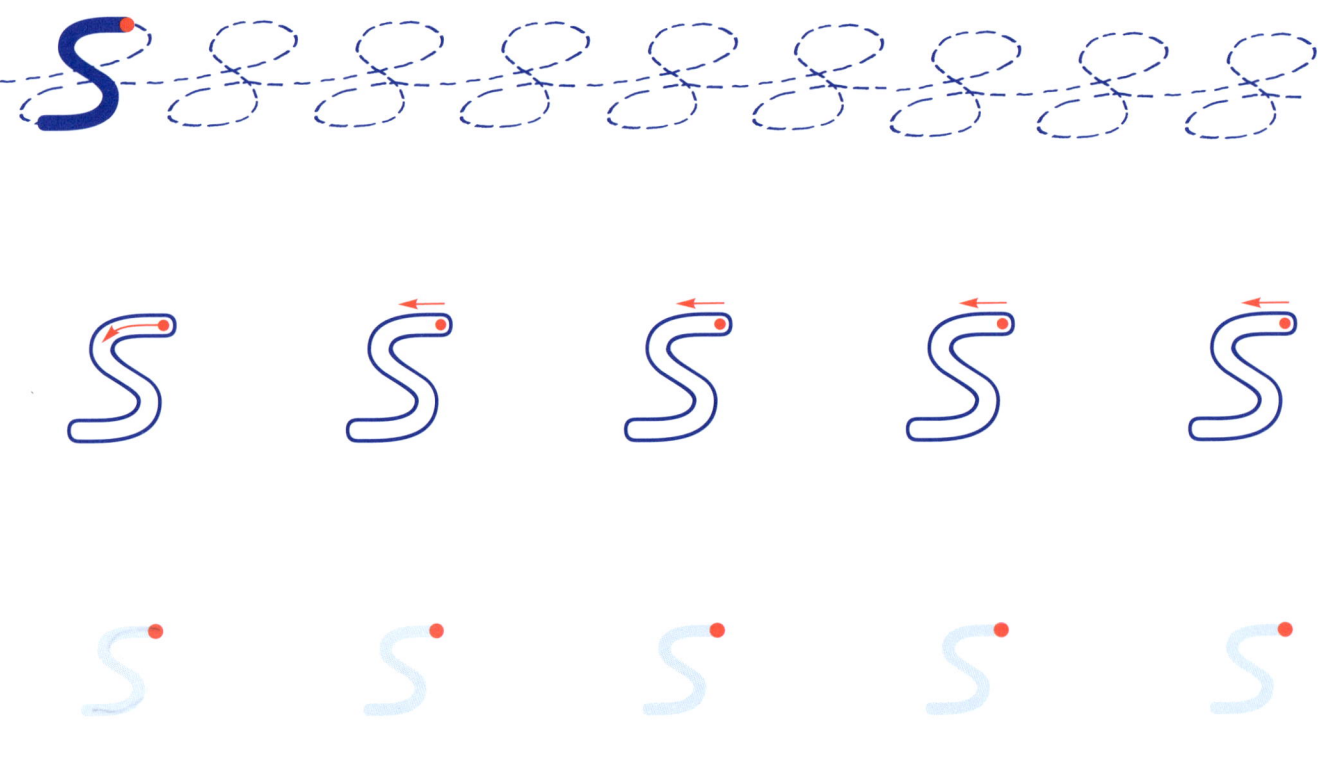

Try your own.

s

a body letter

snake

one sun

1 1 1

1 1 1

1 1 1

two wheels

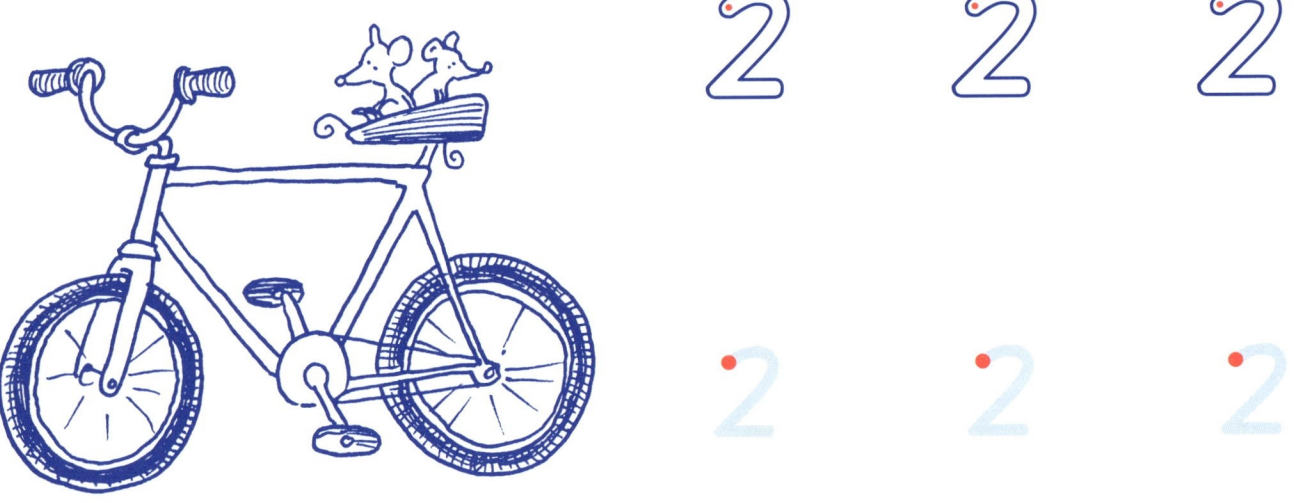

2 2 2

2 2 2

2 2

three children on a see-saw

3 3 3 3

3 3 3

3 3 3 • • •

four legs on a giraffe

4 4 4 4

4 4 4 4

4

five rings on a hand

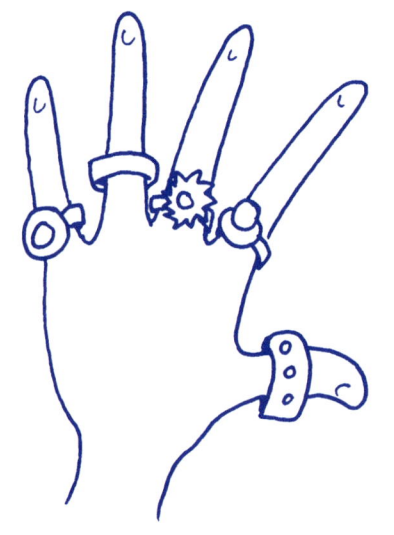

5 5 5 5

5 5 5 5

5 5 5 · · ·

six legs on an insect

6 6 6 6

6 6 6 6

6 6 6 · · ·

seven dwarfs

7 7 7 7 7 7

7 7 7 7 7 7

eight legs on an octopus

8 8 8

8 8 8

8 8 8

nine wheels

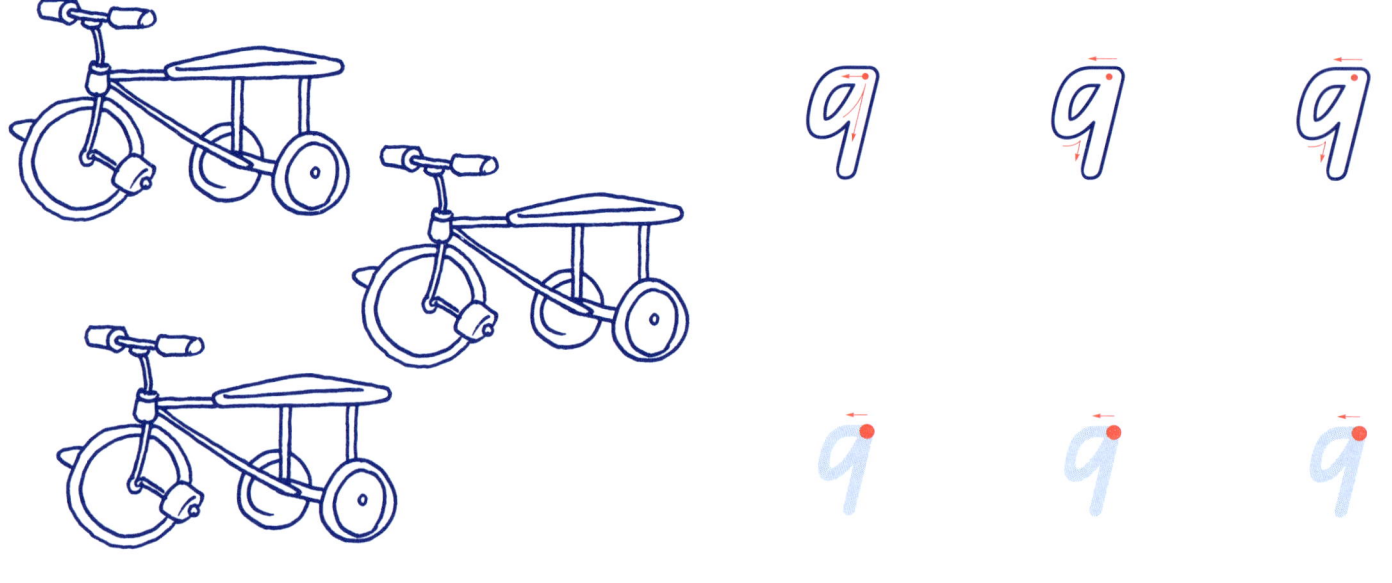

9 9 9

9 9 9

9 9 9 • • •

ten toes

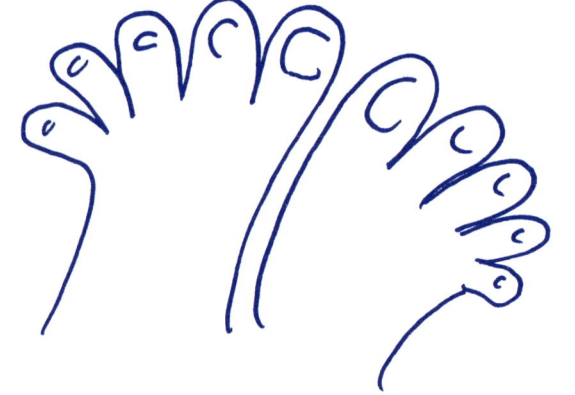

10 10 10

10 10 10 10 10 10

10 10 10 • • • • • •